"Eric Maisel has devoted his life to sharing his deep understanding of creativity, meaning, and life purpose. In this new book, Maisel explores the suffering of smart people and once again offers innovative paradigms and practical solutions to end their pain."

—Gail McMeekin, author of *The 12 Secrets of Highly Creative Women* and *The 12 Secrets of Highly Successful Women*

"In this insightful examination of the challenges bright individuals face, Eric Maisel explores how to reclaim your passion and to live a richer and more productive life. It's a smart move to read this wise book."

—John Moir, author of *Return of the Condor: The Race to Save Our Largest Bird from Extinction*

"If you're so smart, why are you in so much pain? Dr. Maisel gets to the root of the special mental challenges of bright people, provides a new system for deriving meaning and joy from life, and helps you conquer the special challenges of being smart with compassionate and invaluable advice! This book will make a smart person even smarter."

—Dr. Katharine Brooks, author of *You Majored in What? Mapping Your Path from Chaos to Career*

"Eric Maisel's *Why Smart People Hurt* is original, provocative, and also reassuring. His conceptualization of mania as a thinking disorder and his treatment for this are original ideas that to my knowledge have never before been expressed. I have taken several courses from Eric and I know personally how powerful his methods are. His principles of natural psychology are, as he describes, simple and yet immensely practical and effective."

—Dr. Laurie Jo Moore, MD, ABPN, FRANZCP

"This is a wise, insightful, and compassionate guide for bright, sensitive, and creative people. If you're smart, you'll get it."

—Michael J. Gelb, author of *How to Think Like Leonardo Da Vinci: Seven Steps to Genius Every Day*

WHY SMART
PEOPLE HURT

OTHER BOOKS BY ERIC MAISEL

NONFICTION

Affirmations for Artists
The Art of the Book Proposal
The Atheist's Way
Become a Creativity Coach Now!
Brainstorm
Coaching the Artist Within
Creative Recovery
The Creativity Book
Creativity for Life
Deep Writing
Everyday You
Fearless Creating
A Life in the Arts
Living the Writer's Life
Making Your Creative Mark
Mastering Creative Anxiety

Natural Psychology
Performance Anxiety
The Power of Sleep Thinking
Rethinking Depression
Sleep Thinking
Ten Zen Seconds
Toxic Criticism
20 Communication Tips at Work
20 Communication Tips for Families
The Van Gogh Blues
What Would Your Character Do?
Write Mind
A Writer's Paris
A Writer's San Francisco
A Writer's Space

FICTION

Aster Lynn
The Blackbirds of Mulhouse
The Black Narc
Dismay
The Fastest Horse Available
The Fretful Dancer

The Kingston Papers
Love in Focus
Murder in Berlin
Murder on Capitol Hill
New Israel

JOURNALS

Artists Speak
Writers and Artists on Devotion
Writers and Artists on Love

MEDITATION DECKS

Everyday Calm
Everyday Creative
Everyday Smart

WHY SMART PEOPLE HURT

A GUIDE FOR THE BRIGHT, THE SENSITIVE, AND THE CREATIVE

ERIC MAISEL

Conari Press

First published in 2013 by Conari Press, an imprint of
Red Wheel/Weiser, LLC
With offices at:
665 Third Street, Suite 400
San Francisco, CA 94107
www.redwheelweiser.com

Library of Congress Cataloging-in-Publication Data

Maisel, Eric, 1947-
  Why smart people hurt : a guide for the bright, the sensitive, and the creative / Eric Maisel.
     pages cm
  ISBN 978-1-57324-626-2
  1. Gifted persons--Psychology. 2. Intellect. I. Title.
  BF412.M32 2013
  153.9'8--dc23
                                    2013017678

Cover design by *www.levanfisherdesign.com*/Barbara Fisher
Interior by Fortuitous
Typeset in Goudy and Solano Gothic

Portions of Chapter 14: The God-Bug Syndrome were previously published
in a slightly different form as "The God Bug Syndrome" in *Psychology
Today*.

Printed in the United States of America
MAL
10 9 8 7 6 5 4 3 2

For Ann, as always

CONTENTS

INTRODUCTION:
THE CHALLENGES OF SMART

Who speaks to the challenges faced by the 1 billion people with a better-than-average ability to think? Who speaks to you?

I hope to do a little of that speaking in this book.

This isn't a book about what smart is or how many people are smart or how many people are really smart. It's a book about the challenges that smart people face, however *smart* is defined and whatever the number of smart people. It is a book about the challenges that you face.

Smartness is a smart person's defining characteristic. Everything she thinks about the world—how she forms her identity, how she construes her needs, how she talks to herself about her life purposes and goals—is a function of how her particular brain operates. She is her smartness in a way that she is not her height, her gender, her moods, or her experiences. Her particular mind with its particular intelligence is the lens through which she looks at life, and it is also the engine that drives her days and her nights. It is her idiosyncratic brain, mind, and intelligence that determine how she will live—and why.

An aspect of her self-awareness is the knowledge that she is smart. She is aware very early on that she is a little or a lot different from the people around her, and this sense of difference—which can be experienced as grand (or grandiose), as alienating, as mortifying, as wonderful, as burdensome—is her abiding sense of herself.

She may also be smart and not quite know it. She may receive so many messages early on about "people like her" not being smart that she may not identify herself as a smart person—while at the same time being one. This painful situation, in which she doubts that she is smart because of her early experiences, is likewise a defining feature of her life. She may as a result make choices "below" her level of smartness while at the same time recognizing that the people who occupy "positions of smartness" above her are no smarter than she is.

We have these many different scenarios to consider. One smart person will be born into a family of smart people where his smartness is identified immediately and where smartness is revered. Another smart person will be born into a family of smart people who have always minimized their own smartness, dislike what they call "putting on airs," and see it as their duty to put him in his place from birth. Each smart person has his own story to tell—and his special challenges to face.

What are those special challenges? Each person experiences different ones, but here are fifteen that many people have in common:

1. Living in a society and a world that disparages smartness

2. Living in a society and a world that does more than disparage smartness, that actually silences smart people (because the power and privilege of leaders is undercut by smart people like you pointing out fraud, illogic, and injustice)

3. Doing work day after day and year after year that fails to make real use of your brainpower

4. Possessing good ideas but, because of the power structure and practices of your work environment, not having a way to implement them

5. Falling prey to physical ailments and bad habits like jaw clenching, head scratching, and cigarette smoking that arise as you try to focus hard on an intellectual or creative problem

6. Feeling alienated from and out of sync with your culture, your family, and your friends

7. Getting trapped in a narrow corner of a field or discipline where you are forced to do repetitive work for a lifetime

8. Finding yourself in a culture that tracks children, thereby keeping late bloomers and children of poverty out of intellectually interesting professions

9. Dealing with a racing brain that, because it doesn't come with an off switch, inclines itself toward insomnia, manias, obsessions, compulsions, and addictions

10. Pining for productive obsessions (juicy intellectual or artistic problems to bite into) but succumbing to unproductive obsessions instead

11. Being smart, but not as smart as you wish you were or need to be

12. Defensively using your brain's ability to reason so as to reduce the anxiety you're experiencing

13. Loving language and getting trapped by certain words and phrases (for example, finding yourself chasing after the great American novel or the missing link)

14. Feeling sadder than other people by virtue of your ability to comprehend the facts of existence

15. Experiencing problems related to meaning because you see through traditional answers about the nature of the universe

This last challenge is especially poignant, which is why I want to introduce you to the principles and practices of natural psychology. For some years, I've been developing natural psychology as a way to update and expand ideas from classical psychology, cognitive-behavioral psychology, and existential psychology. Natural psychology takes as its starting point the question, what exactly is meaning? This is a question of real concern to smart people.

Natural psychology identifies meaning first as a subjective psychological experience, second as a certain sort of idea that we form, and third as a certain sort of evaluation about life that we hold. It then describes the profound shift that a person can experience from seeking meaning to making meaning and distinguishes between making meaning any which way and value-based meaning-making. It further identifies making meaning as *the* key to emotional health and personal satisfaction.

We might start our exploration by looking at what happens right from the beginning of life when a bright child is born into a family or society where being smart is underappreciated or disparaged. We might begin by trying to get a handle on what sort of thing being a smart person is by looking at some of the threats that come from a racing mind—threats like mania, insomnia, obsessions, and addictions. But I'd like us to start with the meaning instead. Here is a report from a client who nicely illustrates our existential themes. Jeanette explained:

> My first negative experience of being too smart was in fifth grade. I had gone to a rural school (a tiny village on the Washington side of the Columbia Gorge) in a three-room school that combined grades since there were very few of us. I was in the largest class (five students). Whether it was intentionally progressive or not, we had stations and were free to roam the room and read or do arithmetic or work on puzzles as we chose. It was heaven.

> Then my family moved to a Portland suburb, and I was in a regimented fifth-grade

class with a Nazi teacher who made us sit with our hands folded if we finished an exercise before the others, which I always did. I learned how excruciating boredom can be; I began to eat sugar to soothe myself, and I acted out. I was in trouble a good deal of the time from then on.

I have always associated my intelligence with a propensity for boredom, for hypervigilance, for hypersensitivity, and a frustrated quest for meaning. Into adolescence, I learned that drama was an antidote to boredom, and then I discovered alcohol, and for the next twenty years, lived in drinking and drama as well as bad relationships that enabled both. However, I do credit my intelligence with helping me to be a highly functional drunk (graduate school, PhD, jobs as a professor, and an ability to look good while under the influence).

When I found myself in a treatment center, the staff apparently had a pool on how long I would stay. Their experience was that the very intelligent were the least trainable into the twelve steps and sobriety. However, I beat those odds and have been sober ever since. However, I still struggle with boredom, with food addiction as a soother, and with workaholism to stay engaged. Fortunately, I found painting and fiction writing as partial answers; and the idea of the necessity of making meaning has been the real lifesaver.

We hear in Jeanette's story many of our themes. We see how boredom arises as a special, terrible problem for smart people. A smart person has a lively brain; that brain wants to work; it is primed to think; and if you give it nothing to do, it will do nothing for as long as it can bear to do nothing, but it will not be happy. It will be bored and, worse, begin to doubt the meaningfulness of life. It will say to itself, "Golly, is this what life is all about, doing a boring job and then maybe watching some television?" A bored smart person is a person smack in the middle of a meaning crisis.

If you were to find yourself in that situation, isn't it reasonable to suppose that you might engage in something at once exciting and soothing to deal with this painful state of affairs? Mightn't you start drinking a lot? Mightn't you drive fast around town? Mightn't you gamble? Mightn't you seek out as much sex as possible? It is easy to see how sadness, obsessions, compulsions, and addictions arise as a response to meaning crises where you find yourself underoccupied, bored, and bereft of the experience of meaning.

We begin to see how, for example, addiction might arise in a bored smart person as a reaction to a meaning problem rather than as a medical problem, a genetic problem, a psychological problem, or a problem with willpower. For example, quite a number of our Nobel Prize–winning novelists have been alcoholics. Is it more likely that they share the same medical problem or that they share the same problems with smartness, boredom, and meaning?

Meaning is primarily a subjective psychological experience. A smart person is more likely than the next person to be aware of its absence and to be affected by its absence. He is more likely to get bored, to experience meaninglessness, to begin to see the extent to which neither his society nor the universe are built to satisfy his meaning needs, and to then hunt for soothing or exciting meaning substitutes that ultimately reduce his freedom.

Meaning is a smart person's most difficult challenge. In natural psychology we say: look to a meaning problem before you look to a medical problem, a psychological problem, or a so-called mental disorder. If you are smart and you do not know what to do to handle meaning crises when they arise, you are in danger of living in perpetual pain.

As a creativity coach and a natural psychology specialist, I talk to smart people every day of the week. I chat with lawyers, doctors, scientists, writers, painters, businesspeople, and folks from every walk of life. They include folks settled in a profession as well as folks struggling to find an outlet for their intelligence and looking for work that will allow them to be as smart as they are. They include individuals who are successful in their careers and those who, because of the realities of the marketplace, struggle to achieve success.

Virtually all of them are bothered by the sadness that dogs so many contemporary intelligent people. Virtually all of them are afflicted by anxiety that is connected to their very ability to think. Many have had to deal with addictions, and many still must deal with them. Some are not strangers to mania, and many live in that stran-gled calm state that smart people cling to so as to avoid actual mania. What they have in common is that they are smart—and in pain.

What they are not necessarily smart about are the challenges of being smart. As likely as not, they have never thought about the fifteen challenges I listed above and therefore have never considered using their native intelligence to meet these challenges. They tend not to realize the extent to which being smart produces its own problems. That is often a considerable part of our work together, laying bare the shadow side of smartness.

It's a difficult territory to talk about because it con-nects to many cultural taboos. We aren't supposed to talk about who might be smarter than whom or what chal-lenges might flow from that smartness. The whole intel-ligence debate is a minefield. But smart people wonder about such things. They wonder, if they are physicists, if they are smart enough to do the big thinking required of them to break through and make a real contribution to science. They wonder, if they are novelists, if they are smart enough to hold all of the themes and threads of their novel in their head. Individuals wonder about these matters even if as a society we can't discuss them.

It certainly isn't the case that smart people as a group have it harder than other people. Smart people are more suited for and more likely to grab society's highest-paying jobs, from doctor to academic to stockbroker, and have a better chance at material ease than other people. We could name countless ways in which smart people have it easier than, or at least no harder than, other people.

Nevertheless smart people encounter many special challenges that can cost them their equanimity, their self-confidence, and their emotional health.

Among these challenges, and the one that I want to explore first because of its vital importance, is the challenge of meaning. This challenge manifests itself in all of the following ways:

- Spending years searching for meaning, not realizing that meaning must be made and not sought

- Never quite ascertaining what meaning investments to make or what meaning opportunities to seize, leaving us with the sense of going through the motions in life

- Doing the work of making meaning but periodically experiencing the meaning drain right out of our activities and enterprises, causing an acute meaning crisis

- Dealing with repetitive or chronic meaning crises via self-soothing activities that turn into obsessions, compulsions, or addictions

- Feeling guilty and upset about engaging in activities that aren't provoking the psychological experience of meaning, not realizing that life does not have to feel constantly meaningful or that a certain amount of time can be lived in meaning neutral without detriment

- Prematurely abandoning activities that might have provoked the psychological experience of meaning down the road

- Experiencing malaise and angst, not realizing that a meaning crisis has struck, and pinning on a convenient label provided by our culture, a label like *clinical depression* or *attention deficit disorder*

- And many more . . .

The primary challenge that smart people must deal with is making sense of meaning. Natural psychology suggests that the best answer to this problem is donning the mantle of meaning-maker and engaging in value-based meaning-making. Your answer may be different, but you must still face this challenge. No smart person is immune to this problem. In fact, it is the most significant emotional issue for our smartest 15 percent.

Do you understand what meaning is, what it isn't, and how to create it? Do you know how to organize your day around meaning investments and meaning opportunities? Are you still searching for meaning after all these years? As long as you continue to experience meaning as a problem, you are bound to suffer from the smart-ache that plagues so many smart people.

We've begun now. I hope I've given you some food for thought. If you'd like to continue thinking about the themes I've raised in this introduction, following are some questions for you to answer.

CHAPTER QUESTIONS

At the end of each chapter, I provide a few thought-provoking questions. If you want to do a little writing on the issues presented, choose one or more questions to address.

Even if you tackle only one question, you will learn a lot about your situation and point yourself in the direction of answers. Remember that answering a question is not the same as taking action. If in your answer you identify certain work that you ought to do, then by all means, do it!

1. What are your first thoughts about the challenges I've identified and how they do or do not apply to you?

2. Do you agree that a smart person is at greater risk for meaning crises?

3. How do you interpret the phrase *value-based meaning-making?*

4. Since meaning is primarily a subjective psychological experience, what do you suppose you can do to create more of it for yourself?

5. How might the very idea of meaning that you create help you deal with meaning crises?

1

SMARTNESS DISPARAGED

Countless infants are born into a social class, ethnic group, religious group, family of origin, or other set of circumstances or environmental factors in which their native intelligence either counts for little or is held as a negative.

Only a few theories of personality, primarily those influenced by Marxist economic ideas, have taken into account the challenges to personality development and expression created by these environmental circumstances. Yet that disparagement and negativity are hugely significant. If you have a good brain and the world you grow up in demands that you shut it down, you are bound to suffer.

Imagine the following sort of day in the life of a young girl with lots of native intelligence. Her household is in chaos, the kind of chaos that poverty, acrimony, addictions, and unfulfilled lives produce. Surrounded by threats, impulsivity, and zero tolerance for free thought, she somehow manages to get to school—and into another anti-thinking environment.

At school, more chaos prevails and, despite the idea that school advocates for thinking, she is confronted with a shrink-wrapped, fact-based, topic-based, and test-driven curriculum that no adult with the freedom to leave would tolerate for an instant.

After school, she goes off to parochial instruction and gets a narrow religious education that demands obedience, allegiance, and more thoughtlessness. Her evening involves her in more chaos, and to escape it she shuts her door, if she is lucky enough to have a room and a door, and finds some stress relief and some self-soothing by watching hours of ready-made, low-level television programming that further numbs her and dumbs her down. Finally she sleeps, only to awaken to another day just like this one.

What will happen to her brain potential in these circumstances? We can imagine. Likely, the best that she can do is bury herself in her books and become a good student, a grade seeker, a dreamer, or a mini-expert in some niche area of thought like spelling or puzzle solving, all of which is a far cry from becoming the deep, free, satisfied thinker she might have become in other circumstances.

That's probably a best-case scenario. More likely, she will not think much, even though she has the ability to think, and when confronted by tasks that require her to think, she will find herself too anxious and too unprepared to meet the rigors of thinking. As a result, she will fail, disappoint herself, dream small, and begin to form an identity that includes a huge doubt about whether she is as smart as she thought she was.

This child is bound to grow sad, bound to act out or to sabotage herself, bound to show the symptoms of one mental disorder or another, from childhood depression to attention deficit disorder to obsessive-compulsive disorder. We may see her try to gain some control of her life through anorexia; we may see her run away, get pregnant early, marry early, try college and drop out, and throughout these years maintain a love-hate relationship with thinking, at once craving it and avoiding it.

A child can't really meet these challenges herself. No six-year-old or nine-year-old or eleven-year-old can change this situation for herself—even if in a corner of her awareness she knows something is seriously wrong, even if she recognizes that there is a better way just out of reach, and even if she tries to stubbornly ignore her environment and entertain dreams and goals for her future.

These negative outcomes are lamentable, but they are also natural. They are exactly what you would expect to see if at every turn you prevented a child from thinking freely and deeply. If you put a good brain in a brain-unfriendly environment, it should not surprise you to see that brain get sad (a state that will eventually be labeled *chronic depression*), respond impulsively and carelessly rather than thoughtfully, doubt its abilities and its options, and choose a station in life a notch or two below the one it might otherwise have chosen.

Let's follow this child and give her a new lease on life, say, when she is twenty-seven, has had to survive the consequences of these environmental challenges and her own spotty past, and comes into contact with a psychology like natural psychology that alerts her to the fact that the place she has arrived is rather to be expected.

The language of natural psychology—with which we talk about original personality, formed personality, and available personality, about meaning investments and meaning opportunities, about the unfortunate but completely normal (as opposed to so-called abnormal or disordered) consequences of environmental challenges, and about distress relief rather than the diagnosis and treatment of mental disorders—can help her think about what has transpired and about what is now required of her if she is to reduce her distress.

In the language of natural psychology, she has an original personality that came with a good brain, a desire to think, and a propensity to think; a formed personality that has had to deal with all the impediments to thinking put in her way and which has dealt with those impediments relatively unsuccessfully; and considerable available personality that possesses an intuitive memory of her original personality and enough awareness of the contours of her formed personality to make real, significant changes.

She can use her available personality to learn how to tolerate the anxiety that now accompanies her efforts at thinking; she can seize thinking as a meaning opportunity and make conscious meaning investments in some thinking domain, whether it's a profession that she thought was out of her reach or a body of knowledge that she would love to study but didn't dare begin for fear of failing herself again. These are the sorts of efforts and changes that she can commence to make.

In addition to learning to deal with the deficits that are part of her formed personality, she can also learn to deal with environmental factors that have not gone away. If she goes back to spend a day with her family, she will again have to deal with that anti-thinking environment. If she has not left her church, she will have to deal with that anti-thinking environment. If her friends sneer at thinking, she will have to deal with them. If she turns on the television to relax, she will have to deal with the anti-thinking programming filling every channel. That she heroically works on herself doesn't prevent environmental factors from continuing their mischief and mayhem.

It is natural and predictable that our environment may pressure us to not think. This pressure will produce pain as we intuit that we are missing out on a native opportunity and will negatively affect our personality, producing everything from math anxiety to depression. If you were born to think and got pushed off that path, then one of your chief jobs, if you want to experience less distress, will be making use of your available personality to craft a new, friendlier relationship with your brain.

A child who grows up in an environment that disparages thinking, that actively works to shut it down at every turn, and that begins to track him and tell him what he is good for and what is beyond his reach, will then find himself in the jaws of his society's work machinery. He will be fit for one sort of job and not another, he will be aimed into one social class and not another, and he will find himself with limited, disappointing options. Here is how Jonathan in England explained it:

I don't know how it works in other countries, but where I live, there is a life-tracking effect in place, where if you happen to be somehow put on the wrong track, as regards your intelligence, it can be a nightmare trying to put it straight later in life.

One of my fellow Mensans complained that she encountered resistance from potential employers because she had been forced to take CSE exams at school instead of the more prestigious O-Level, even though she had later gone on to acquire the professional certifications necessary for her chosen career.

It cannot simply be left up to a young school dropout who has been mistracked and educationally disserviced, and who has been let loose on the world of industry, to now suddenly redevelop the self-esteem that has been robbed from her, to expect her to solve her finances (probably by now on an entry-level job in the service industry) so she can go to college and make it through a degree program as if everything had all been fine and dandy.

It can take years to recover from such a mauling, and even when the emotional and personal side of things is resolved, there is still the matter of no degree and no proper career. Unfortunately, industry and academia both act as if the highest level of educational attainment that was available to a person when young represents the maximum worth of their mind. That's kind of tough when it wasn't your fault.

There needs to be more help for adults in such situations, perhaps via fast-track apprenticeship programs, so that they can get into suitable careers. Many of us in this situation actually read and study a great deal independently and so don't want to sit through classes just for certification. The unresolved situation in my case is a lack of a suitable career that taps in to my interests and aptitudes. I am getting older and remain a highly gifted autodidact unsuccessfully searching for a job in the neurosciences.

A smart person has a desire to think, a need to think, and an ability to think. But the nature of family, school, and work; the structure of society; and the proclivities of the people around him often conspire to put out his intellectual fire.

His family is unlikely to inspire him or flame his desire to think; school is unlikely to inspire him; his job is unlikely to inspire him; his pastor is unlikely to inspire him; mass entertainment and his other relaxations are unlikely to inspire him; the uninteresting conversations around him are unlikely to inspire him.

He can't help but recognize the headline truth about his life and his environment: "Little thinking allowed here." Yet he may be surprised to learn just how deep this antipathy runs. In fact, in most societies thought is not just disparaged; the thinking person is targeted as an enemy of the people. He is mocked as elitist and effete, his progressive views are hated, and if he lives in a society run by tyrants, he will be silenced and may be imprisoned or murdered.

Tyrants hate intellectuals, for intellectuals as a class see tyranny for what it is and can articulate what they see. They know when freedom is being violated and stolen. They are better attuned to knowing that they are being fed lies. They recognize to what extent the majority opinion is an anti-intellectual one.

Attacks on thinking and attacks on smart people occur all the time. Here is one report from contemporary Iraq, as reported by the watchdog group A Face and a Name: Civilian Victims of Insurgent Groups in Iraq:

> Some Iraqi academics see the current attacks as a way to destroy Iraq's intellectual elite. Precise figures are difficult to obtain, but studies suggest that doctors and academics are particularly at risk. A study by the Iraqi Ministry of Health concluded that armed groups have abducted between 160 and 300 Iraqi doctors since April 2003, and killed more than twenty-five. Nearly 1,000 doctors have fled the country, the study said, with an average of thirty more following each month. To stem the outflow, the ministry broadcast a public service announcement on television

in spring 2005, with a message that said: 'Dear Citizens, please do not kill doctors— you may need them one day.'

Professors at Iraq's once prestigious universities are also under attack. According to an April 2005 United Nations University report, assassins have killed forty-eight academics since 2003, and many more teachers and professors brave daily threats. Hundreds of academics and professionals have been threatened with death and told to leave Iraq. According to the Association of University Teachers, 2,000 professors have left Iraq since 2003, joining the 10,000 professors the association says left the country in the twelve years after the Gulf War.

Attacks on people who can think occur in every culture and in every epoch. Rebellious feminists in Russia are labeled with mental disorders made up on the spot for the purposes of incarcerating them. Scientists who point out the environmental dangers caused by business are ridiculed as fear mongers. Every age and every culture has its versions of cultural revolutions, inquisitions, and Scopes trials.

It is impossible for a child who is born smart to have any inkling that her abilities are likely to be disparaged, that thinking itself will be envied and hated by some in her society, or that she may be targeted by her government because she has chosen a thinking profession. What smart child building with blocks or surfing the Net could possibly suspect how unfriendly her species is to thinking and to the fruits of thinking like science, culture, and freedom? Such a notion would make no sense to her. Yet those are the abiding truths about our species that perennially contribute to the distress that smart people experience.

CHAPTER QUESTIONS

1. Was your smartness disparaged as you were growing up?

2. What messages did you receive about your capabilities and talents?

3. What messages did you receive about whether it was admirable or unseemly to be smart?

4. If you received mixed messages about your smartness, what was the bottom line or ultimate message?

5. Given that those messages and that upbringing necessarily influenced your formed personality, what do you need to do *now* to recover your rightful smartness?

2

SMART WORK AS OXYMORON

We can imagine a situation far back in time in which nothing in a person's life could be singled out as one's profession or line of work. If you had to grow or catch your own food, make your own clothes, dream up your own metaphors for the night sky, heal your own injuries, make your own love matches, concoct your own stimulants and sedatives, and in every way imaginable take care of yourself and amuse yourself, you had no profession or line of work. You were simply living; you were simply a human being.

You weren't a baker or a homebuilder or a utensil maker or a natural philosopher; you were all those things. Now such a life is virtually impossible. While you can be several things—a lawyer during the day and a painter on Sunday; a grocer during the day, a cabinet maker in the evening, and a fisherman on the weekend; and so on—there is an undeniable sense in which our species has sorted itself into jobs, professions, and lines of work.

Smart people, if they get the chance or make the chance, will find themselves needing to choose from among a standard menu of work opportunities with names like doctor, lawyer, teacher, scientist, novelist, entrepreneur, and so on. Each job on this list may hold some cachet in society, but each may also hold no meaning for a given smart individual. The sorting out of society's needs creates jobs and professions—some of which putatively allow for thinking, many of which do not—but that very sorting reduces the chances that a given smart individual can find a line of work that feels genuinely meaningful.

There is no necessary connection between the value that society puts on a line of work and its meaningfulness to a given individual. Society may hold the profession of doctor in high esteem, but if you do not find medicine a meaningful line of work, it is not meaningful to you. Society may not hold the profession of elementary school teacher in high esteem (whatever lip service it may pay to the value and importance of that work), but if you find that a meaningful line of work, then it is meaningful to you. To repeat a central fact about meaning and a core teaching in natural psychology, meaning is a subjective psychological experience. If certain work isn't meaningful to you, it simply isn't.

This problem is compounded by the following additional reality. People do not become lawyers, doctors, or scientists. They become corporate lawyers or litigators, pediatricians or brain surgeons, geologists or physicists. That is, people are forced to specialize—and that specializing typically further reduces the meaningfulness of that line of work. Maybe practicing law might have proven meaningful if you had not also wanted to make money and had chosen poverty law instead of corporate law. Maybe science might have proven meaningful if you could have stepped back to look at the biggest issues rather than having to drill down into a niche where you work with one organism, one atomic particle, or one geological formation. But the way that professional work is constituted nowadays, you are bound to have to specialize.

There is no contemporary category of *general thinker* that matches the ancient job title of *natural philosopher*, in which people could do science, philosophy, art, and anything else that caught their fancy. Smart people today must become clear somethings—college professors specializing in the early works of Melville, engineers specializing in bridges, lawyers who know tax law, and so on—and, having become that something, *must stay right there*, trapped with the duty of preparing another journal article, pondering another bend in the river, or familiarizing themselves with another tax code change.

Marilyn, a biological researcher, explained:

> The journey to get where I am today as a biological researcher at a prestigious university was long and hard, and because it was so hard, with so many hurdles to jump over and hoops to jump through, I never noticed exactly what was happening. I never noticed that in some of my undergraduate classes, I was actually excited by the material and actually enjoyed thinking about the big questions but that as each year progressed and as I had to narrow my focus, find my niche, and

choose my life form, as it were (I've ended up an expert on a certain worm), I stopped thinking and spent my days in pretty dreary fashion trying to find some enthusiasm for my own research. Biology is amazing—I am a biologist—and yet it has all come together in a very disappointing way.

Martin, a professor of philosophy, described his situation:

I've spent the last two months defending a journal article I wrote about praise and blame in Kantian ethics from the three peer reviewers who nitpicked my article to death. In order to have a chance to get it published, I need to address every one of their concerns—and the problem for me isn't so much that I'm spending all of my time on what feels like a silly and mind-numbing task but rather that this is the box I've put myself in, this exact box, where I make some fine logical or linguistic distinctions and then have to act like that matters, like I am increasing human knowledge or something.

The academy is a comfortable place to be, and I suppose I could turn myself into someone who does think bigger than I currently think. Maybe I can't really blame the system. But if I don't blame the system, then I would have to look in the mirror—which, by the way,

Why Smart People Hurt

Kant would have called a praiseworthy act, as for him, it was important that we praise that which we find difficult to do. You see that I could write about Kant all day. . . .

I don't know what the problem is: if it is the system, if it is philosophy itself that I don't believe in, if it's a lack of genuine interest in thinking, if it's a lack of confidence, if it's a lack of necessary arrogance, if it's a fear of biting off more than I can chew, or what. Can I really do this for twenty or thirty more years? That seems completely unbearable.

Professions and lines of work as they are currently constituted come with countless challenges. Most do not actually make much room for thinking. They look like thinking professions, but day in and day out, they may amount to something considerably duller instead. Maybe you find yourself in what you consider a really interesting corner of evolutionary biology working on enriching the concept of fitness. But what are you actually doing on a daily basis? Moving cultures from one controlled environment to another controlled environment and taking measurements. That is the nature of the beast, but can it provoke the psychological experience of meaning?

Genetic drift is one of the mechanisms of evolution. It is an important aspect of human existence and an interesting subject to study. But as important and interesting as it is, if you find yourself researching in a corner of genetic drift, perhaps researching some group analogous to the

Bounty sailors and their Pitcairn Island experience to see if the group you've chosen also manifests the reduction of genetic diversity you would expect to find in such situations, you may find yourself quite bored. The concept is powerful, the subject is interesting, and your research is logical—yet it may amount to a yawn.

Can you know this growing up as you look out at the world of jobs and professions? How could you? You are probably going to do your best to shy away from jobs that allow for little or no thinking. Except under dire circumstances or as a day job to support creative endeavors, a smart person is not so likely to want to wait tables, file forms, work on an assembly line, or sell shoes. It isn't that he disparages these lines of work as beneath his dignity; rather, it is that he can see clearly how his days would be experienced as meaningless if he had to spend his time not thinking. But as well as you may know what you don't want to do, how clearly will you be able to gauge what you *do* want to do?

As a smart person growing up, you're likely to consider many of the traditional smart professions or be told that you ought to consider them. Casually mention that you might like a microscope for Christmas and you may be on your way to a job in the sciences whether or not you actually find scientific research meaningful. Get an A on a short story and that may mark you forever as someone who ought to write, even if your genuine loves are music and cooking. We've already discussed how your intelligence may be disparaged as you grow up. On top of that, the apparatus of society and the natural progression of life from childhood to adulthood will force you to pick some work—work that you can't really visualize and that may prove much less interesting and meaningful than you expected.

Let's tie some of these threads together. The themes of our first three chapters—that how a smart person construes meaning matters, that a smart person's smartness is often disparaged, and that a smart person comes into the world with an original personality that then collides with that world—come together in the following report. Jack, a lawyer-turned-actor, explained:

> In my own case, I must admit that I was blessed with two very intelligent parents. My mother chose to remain at home while my father was the sole breadwinner. I have four older brothers who are considerably older than me (I think I was an "oops" baby). My parents were younger and I believe more hands-on with my older brothers, and with that attention came great expectations. By the time I reached school age, my parents were either too tired to care or perhaps they had mellowed as far as expectations went.
>
> Consequently, my oldest brother *had to* bring home straight-A report cards, but when I brought my own report cards home, my parents would ask me, "Are you happy with this result?" I'd shrug and they'd reply, "Well, as long as you're happy." Oddly enough, this reaction didn't make me happy. Actually, it

left me rather confused and uncertain since I knew my grades didn't come close to what my older brothers achieved, but it gave me permission to do what I wanted to do, which was to complete all my schoolwork during school hours and then spend all of my free time playing outside or watching television.

My brothers were all encouraged to develop their own musical talents in a classic school band setting. When I was old enough to play an instrument, someone decided that I should learn how to play the drums since my older brothers played brass instruments. The thing I couldn't seem to make my family realize was that I hated the drums. I didn't have any sense of rhythm. So I endured years of this torture before I was mercifully allowed to drop music altogether.

The thing was, I never knew that I actually had choices in life. My older brothers all went to university. I thought everyone went to university. I was so surprised when my father informed me that I didn't have to go into sciences if I didn't want to. I then suddenly switched from sciences to arts, but I had no idea what I was to do with my life. And then two of my older brothers went through law school and became lawyers. It became assumed by my family that I would naturally follow their path. I took the LSAT but didn't come close to what my brothers scored when they took it. Consequently, though I submitted the expected application to law school, I was fairly certain I would not be accepted.

When I started considering my options, I finally admitted that I felt incredibly drawn to acting. I was also attracted to writing, but a few choice comments made innocently by my father had squelched any confidence I might have had about my writing. But acting . . . it was something I thoroughly enjoyed and even proved to have some talent for. I applied and was accepted to a Bachelor of Fine Arts in Acting program at my university. One month later, I received a call from the admissions secretary for the law school that I'd applied to, saying I'd been accepted.

Naturally, thinking only of how happy it would make my father and brothers (my mother had died by this point), I dropped out of the theater program and took my seat in law school. I made it through and got my law degree but was then convinced by my older brothers to take the next step, namely take the bar exams. "Once you're a lawyer, they can never take that away from you," they said. My father impressed upon me that at least I would have something to fall back on.

When I completed my training, passed the bar exams, and became a lawyer, I still felt that I was meant to take a different path.

I was all set to audition for the acting program again, but then I was set up on a blind date by one of my older lawyer brothers. Rather rashly, I became infatuated with my date and then allowed myself to be convinced by my new girlfriend that she would not be willing to wait for me to establish myself as an actor. She loved material things, and that need had to be fed. I abandoned my dream and accepted a life as a lawyer.

Though my heart wasn't in it, I would have to say I was a fairly decent lawyer. I rationalized my choice to work in small law firms as opposed to the huge wealthy law firms my brothers worked in. I even set up my own law practice. All the while, I started to die inside. It got to where I knew I had only a few short months left to live, so I discovered I had a backbone and that I could *choose* what I wanted out of life. I got divorced, closed my law practice, and embarked on a path to become a professional actor.

Do I feel that I have failed to meet expectations, or that I have met them (just), or that I exceeded expectations? Quite frankly, I don't care. I feel I am in the right place, doing what feels right for me. My lawyer older brothers make as much in one billable hour as I do in a typical month. I don't own a house anymore, I paid a huge financial penalty for closing my practice, and I now live in a subsidized apartment just getting by. But if I had remained a lawyer making lots of money, I would have been dead a decade ago. I don't feel I need to prove anything to anyone at this point.

The challenges that smart people face when it comes to finding meaningful employment, surviving dull, routine work, avoiding a lifetime in a claustrophobic corner of a profession, choosing between work that pays and work that interests them, and generally adapting their smarts to the contours of society's configurations are worth a book in themselves. You may prove one of the lucky ones and make a beautiful match. More likely, however, you will find yourself among the majority of smart people who perennially find the world of work to be a problem.

CHAPTER QUESTIONS

1. Can work ever feel meaningful? If so, what do you suspect are the necessary conditions for work to provoke the psychological experience of meaning?

2. What work have you found meaningful?

3. Since much work in the service of meaning, like licking envelopes for a good cause, does not itself feel meaningful, how do you intend to treat boring work accomplished in the service of meaning?

4. What new work might constitute a meaning opportunity?

5. What loves from your childhood might be turned into contemporary meaningful work?

3

ORIGINAL, FORMED, AND AVAILABLE PERSONALITIES

Each of us comes into the world with a unique mix of aptitudes, characteristics, inclinations, genetic information, aspects of temperament, and other qualities and capacities that in natural psychology we call "original personality." You are not born a blank slate; no parent believes that nor does anyone who has seen a litter of kittens. Your original personality includes everything from your native intelligence to your basic mood structure and all those aspects of temperament (like adaptability, sensitivity, and distractibility) that developmental psychologists study.

There was a time when people thought that fully a quarter of the human race was born melancholic. It is not unreasonable to suppose that people are born happier or sadder, just as they are born smarter or less smart. Likewise, it is reasonable to suppose that each individual is already born with a certain worldview—or primed for a certain worldview. Probably we are born with sets of both qualities and capacities and also with a unique blue-print—one that may haunt us as a ghostly memory if and when life deflects us from who we might have been or who we ought to have been.

There is nothing surprising about the idea that we are born with an original personality. What is surprising is that, except for a very limited exploration of that cluster of traits known in psychology as temperament—an exploration that, by the way, the helping side of psychology makes almost no use of—all psychologies have avoided thinking about original personality. Psychology does not credit human beings with an original personality or take it into account when psychologists diagnose and treat their clients or patients. Doesn't it matter whether or not the person across from you came into the world already naturally sad if you are going to pin on him the label of *clinically depressed?* Of course it does.

Picture a litter of kittens. One is more curious than the next. One is more aggressive than the next. One is a leader, and another is a follower. The first is not potentially curious; she is *already* curious. The second is not potentially aggressive; he is *already* aggressive. The third and the fourth are not potentially leaders and followers; they are already that. In exactly the same way a human infant is not potentially smart; he is already smart. True, he doesn't have language yet; true, his environment can dumb him down; true, he can't write *War and Peace* or solve quadratic equations. But he is already built a certain way and already looks out at life with a particular mind-set and apparatus.

A smart person is smart right from the beginning.

Then comes the environment. The child looks out at the world with his original personality, interacts with the world according to his original personality, and has his developmental blueprint altered by the world, producing his formed personality. He forms or doesn't form secure attachments, his world is safer or more dangerous, he sees an array of options or few options, and so on. To take a simple analogy, our curious kitten in a loving household becomes a gentle cat but if thrown out into the world, becomes feral. Her curiosity manifests one way in that loving home and another way if she must fend for herself in back alleys. In one environment, it keeps her amused; in another, it helps her kill.

To say this simply, a person's original personality is altered into his formed personality through the circumstances of living. This complex alteration may produce a weakened or a strengthened person, a smarter or a less smart person, an open or a defended person, and so on. Your formed personality may be more than as well as less than your original personality, or more in some regards and less in others. Maybe you were born selfish—not so unusual for a creature with selfish genes—and nevertheless learned generosity. Or maybe your selfishness grew into everyday narcissism. Either is possible, although it is rather the rule that for most people their formed personality will be less than their original personality, since living is a hard game that tends not to bring out the best in us.

All the while, some free personality remains available to us. To use the language of natural psychology, we are born with an original personality, grow into our formed personality through living, and retain available personality—that amount of awareness that allows us to make changes, see our formed personality for what it is, make guesses about our original personality, and, most importantly, set a meaning-making agenda. It is with our available personality that we say, "I am not a slave to my upbringing, and I can make myself proud through my efforts."

You may have been born sad, and life may have made you sadder: it is with your available personality that you deal with that reality.

You may have been born anxious, and life may have made you more anxious: it is with your available personality that you deal with that reality.

You may have been born smart and forced into dumb work: it is with your available personality that you deal with that reality.

The more defensive you are, the less your available personality. The more addicted you are, the less your available personality. The less you think for yourself, the less your available personality. The more the engine of your brain has gone off racing on its own, the less your available personality. The more you've succumbed to one lure or another—we'll examine four lures later on: the lures of language, logic, fantasy, and mysticism—the less your available personality. The more you are being fooled or ruled, the less your available personality.

In short, we may possess much less available personality than we wish we had—and we may know that and experience that as pain.

The following report from Maxine does a lovely job of tying some of these themes together. Maxine explained:

I've done animal rescue for years. Currently I have a feral cat and her litter of three kitties in my attic. It took almost three months for me to see the kitties because she's taught them that the sight and sound of humans is a dangerous thing. I know that I have only their available personality to work with, which even after just a few months is a very fixed and reduced amount. I bet if I could've handled them within days of their being born and played with them in the early weeks, they would've expressed their original personality to me. But as it is, their mama did what she considers a mighty fine job at forming their personalities; and she has very limited skills herself. So every day I just show up, I work with what's available, and original and formed don't really matter. I meet them where they are. There's a beauty in that simplicity and a real honoring of these cats.

But it's all very different when it comes to me. When it comes to dealing with rescue animals with behavior problems, I accept that they have only what's available. It's the sanest approach, because thinking about their lost innocence or what they might have been is devastating to me, and I don't need to be devastated. But if I think about me—or about a friend or a family member—I can't maintain that same neutrality. I grieve for what's been lost. I rebel at the idea that this is all that's left or that this is all that's available. I see and feel the diminishment.

Why do I lose the beauty and simplicity of saying, "Hey, here's what's available today?" Why do I feel paralyzed when I begin thinking about what I should have been or about what life should have been? The idea of available personality goes from feeling useful, simple, and beautiful when it comes to working with rescue animals to feeling like a prison sentence when I apply it to me. I bet I'm not the only one who feels this way. It may be true that we only have so much available personality left to us, but I don't really find that truth acceptable.

A child is born; he is already somebody. To pick one set of circumstances, let's say that he is a bright boy born into a middle-class family that demands good grades and promotes a worldview that includes playing musical instruments, playing sports, admiring nature, going to college, and getting a good job.

The parents pay lip service to the idea that thinking is a good thing but do not do much thinking themselves and do not really like it when their son thinks. They pay lip service to the idea that family members should love

Why Smart People Hurt

one another but don't love much and aren't very warm or friendly. They likewise pay lip service to the ideals of freedom but present their son with the clear message that he is not free to get mediocre grades, not free to dispute their core beliefs, and not free to really be himself.

Of course, this all confuses him. In this environment, he becomes sadder than he was born to be, saddened by having to perform at piano recitals that don't interest him and that make him woefully anxious, saddened by having to take his boring classes seriously, saddened by his parents' inability to love him or take an interest in him, saddened by what he learns in school about how human beings treat one another, and saddened most of all by his inability to make sense of this picture of life—a picture that everyone seems to be holding as the way to live but that to him feels odd, contradictory, empty, and meaningless.

His anxiety at piano recitals is noticed, and he is put on antianxiety medication. His restlessness in class is noticed, and he is put on anti-ADHD medication. His sadness is noticed, and he is put on antidepressants. Now, to go along with his sense that this can't really be the way that life is supposed to feel or be lived, he has three mental disorder labels and three sets of medications that make him a perpetual patient and that produce all sorts of side effects. Everyone in his family seems to think that it is normal that he has three mental disorders—they, of course, all have theirs as well.

Then come his teenage years. Teenagers in first-world countries are underutilized by their society and strangled by the nothingness of school. No amount of tennis lessons, spring vacations, camping trips, or extracurricular activities—including sex, drugs, and rock and roll—can fill the void created by having nothing asked of them. There are only two solutions to this epidemic problem that causes the havoc of Columbine High tragedies, anorexia, teenage suicide, careless sex, video game addiction, social media frenzy, brand name fixation, and deep sadness—that society ask something of its teenagers or that teenagers ask something of themselves. But nothing is asked of this young man except that he do what he is told to do and that he get ready for college.

Somewhere along the line, he begins to have feelings about what work he might like to do and what work he doesn't want to do. His parents—troubled themselves, anxious themselves, with their own opinions and agendas—add their input and try to influence his decision. Since he seems to like biology, why shouldn't he become a doctor? He shrugs, not wanting to think about the future; what he really wants to do is listen to music, watch movies, spend time with his friends, and find a girlfriend.

College comes, and he is obliged to act like he is deciding about his future. His classes are not meaningful to him, and he has trouble not wallowing in sadness. He manages to graduate, and the part-time job he takes one summer as an intern in a large corporation leads oddly and inexorably to a full-time, entry-level job in the corporate world. His early twenties pass in a characteristic haze of happy hour drinking, escapades and infatuations, office politics, and relentless sadness.

In his mid-twenties, he gets lucky. At that point, having had to survive the consequences of his environmental challenges and his own spotty past, he comes into contact with a psychology like natural psychology that alerts him to the fact that the place he has arrived is rather to be expected. Now he has a pivotal choice to make: whether or not to make use of his available personality to reduce his distress and begin making meaning.

He begins to see that the language of natural psychology—in which we talk about original personality, formed personality, and available personality; about meaning investments and meaning opportunities; about the unfortunate but completely normal (as opposed to abnormal or disordered) consequences of environmental challenges, and about distress relief rather than diagnosis and treatment for mental disorders—can help him think about what is now required of him if he is to reduce his distress and right his ship.

He readies himself to deal with all of this. But there is still the problem of his meaningless work. It is one thing to accept the challenge of making meaning, but how exactly does that relate to the world of work? A serious challenge that loomed early on and grew more pressing as he moved from high school through college and into his young adult years was the necessity of choosing a line of work. What young person understands that jobs and professions do not exist to serve his meaning needs and that whatever choice he makes is unlikely to really satisfy? Now he is beginning to understand that.

Challenged to feel less sad, challenged to deal with what is at once an inflated and deflated sense of himself, challenged to actually manifest his smartness, and in pain on many fronts despite his new understanding of life, he must still pay the rent and buy groceries. As much as he might like to, he can't put the matter of work on a back burner. He is forced to grapple with that tedious, slippery, unrelenting challenge that we look at next: the world of work.

CHAPTER QUESTIONS

1. Do you have the sense that you can intuit your original personality? If so, what were its contours? Who do you feel you were supposed to be?

2. What are the major characteristics of your formed personality?

3. Which of those are strengths, and which of those are more like liabilities?

4. If you would like a personality update, describe that update.

5. What do you see as the relationships among your original, formed, and available personalities?

4

OUR EXPERIMENTAL MODEL

Human beings are products of nature, and nature neither does nor can aim for perfection. *Perfection* is not a word that makes sense in the context of evolution. Nature merely tries things out—that is all it can do. It allows life to evolve, which is a lovely, process-oriented way to produce not perfection but endless variety. It tries out this fly and that fly, this virus and that virus. Some endure, some vanish, and each in its own way is merely yet another of nature's experiments.

We are not designed.

Nature creates a creature like us, gives us a super-sized, experimental brain, and tries out thinking. What a fascinating capacity with which to aid or burden a creature! Since the goal of nature is not to create perfection but rather to create functionality within a context, you would naturally expect an immense, wild, and flawed capacity like thinking to come with a set of profound repercussions and challenges. That is indeed what we see—and it's a sort of proof that we are not designed but rather have evolved into existence.

If you suppose that you are created by design and created well, then, like any good machine, each of your parts would have a clear design purpose and would function admirably. If, by contrast, you believe that you are a member of a species that has evolved and that you have been made by the forces of nature and not by a designer's hand, then you have much less reason to be sanguine about the excellent functionality of your brain. It is simply another experiment among nature's billions—and how many experiments actually pan out?

Complicated experiments like us are bound to produce countless unintended consequences and functional shortfalls. It is one thing to evolve a spoon—you will likely do a pretty good job of it and might even succeed on the first try. It is another thing to evolve a blender/mixer that can turn fruit into smoothies and also knead bread dough. Experimentation will naturally produce many excellent spoons and also produce many blenders that don't mix well as well as many mixers that don't blend well. In one, the motor will prove powerful enough to blend but not powerful enough to knead; in another, the bread hook will prove the wrong shape to create a dough ball; and so on.

This is likewise true of the experiment that is our species. Our apposite thumb perhaps works nicely, like any good spoon might, but our brain? As fancy and complicated as it is, does it work that well? We have the brainpower and the brain style that we have, running across a spectrum of capacities and embedded in a spectrum of personalities. For each individual, his or her experimental brain may work beautifully in some circumstances and in some applications and less well in other circumstances and in other applications. This is exactly what we see.

Because it is maybe the most complicated component of the most complicated experiment nature has yet tried, our brain will naturally produce many artifacts and inadvertent consequences. It may, for example, produce a desire to do certain intellectual work that in fact it isn't capable of doing. That is, it may produce a smart gap. It may, for the sake of ease and survival, reduce its understanding of the world to slogans that do not match up with the complexity of reality. It may spin out of control or find itself held hostage to some unimportant worry that can't be shaken.

Perhaps the next model will do better.

But perhaps no model can effectively do what a brain is supposed to do. Once you let a brain think and allow it to try to predict its future and its place in the universe, once you give it meaning needs and identity needs and relational needs and ego needs—once, that is, you put it in what may be an untenable relationship to the facts of existence, what bit of organic matter can really do much with such implausible demands? It is not just that our brain is an experimental model. It has also been given impossible tasks. To take just one example, predicting the future is a necessary part of its game, and the best model imaginable still wouldn't be equal to that impossible challenge.

We have gotten it into our heads that our species is both the final model and equal to its tasks. Neither is necessarily or logically true, and the evidence of our eyes suggests the opposite. Of course, we can't wait for the next model; nor in many important senses can we change our tasks. But we can take a kinder view of our species, as one not built well enough to handle what it has been tasked to handle, and also a tougher view, demanding of our species that it look at its shortfalls and do what it can to rise above them.

Can we do this? Can we take this tougher view and actually do a better job? How good a job should we expect our experimental brain to do as it tries to distinguish between genuine appetites and psychological cravings or between concern and overconcern? Maybe we can expect it to master basic literacy, if it is given a chance at learning, but should we expect it to see through a sophisticated advertising campaign designed to send it to war? Why do we suppose that our brain can look into the future and pick a profession that it will actually love and enjoy for decades—or, perhaps more poignantly, even know what to do with itself for the next fifteen minutes? How well can brains do these things?

We have taken for granted the idea that our brain is equal to life's challenges. But on the one hand the challenges may be too great, and on the other hand our brain may not be designed adequately. As it presently stands, nature has created a brain that thinks it can perform frankly impossible tasks. We have evolved with the ability to tax our brain with questions and challenges that it can't be expected to handle—and then to stand surprised when we see phenomena like, to name two that we'll investigate shortly, mania and insomnia.

What might we like to see in the next model?

Maybe that we come built with an off switch? That would be useful.

Maybe more brain capacity across the board? That might be nice.

Maybe that we think best under pressure—as opposed to what is currently true, namely the exact opposite? That would certainly help at test time.

Maybe that intelligence is not distributed so widely, so that we might all be in it together, thinking the same way?

There is no harm at playing imaginary evolutionary futurist. But if we had the job for real, we would have to ask and try to answer some very hard questions. We'd start with: What goals do we have in mind? Are we thinking of what would improve the life of a given individual (whatever we might mean by *improve*), or are we contemplating what would be most likely to ensure that our species survives? For example, a worldwide tyranny might guarantee that the species would never wipe itself out through nuclear war, since all the weapons would be in the hands of one tyrant. So you might have limited freedom and tremendous terror but also a very robust, vibrant species from an evolutionary point of view. The species might be happy even if none of its members are.

And how might we plan for or predict net gain? Any change has the potential to produce both positive and negative consequences for a species. When a mosquito infestation in the south of France caused the French government to launch a massive campaign of insecticide spraying, the mosquito population shrank dramatically until those mosquitoes resistant to the insecticide had

the chance to grow in numbers. But those resistant mosquitoes turned out to be easier prey for spiders than their
forebears were. They were more resistant to insecticide
and also less adept at avoiding spiders. This is the way of
nature, and how could anyone predict such things?

So we must pity our imaginary evolutionary futurist
his job. But our job is simpler. It is to look at this exact
brain in a naturalistic context with an understanding that
it is not the best it can be but simply an evolved, imperfect contraption. It does not come with an off switch that
might allow it to get a good night's sleep every single
night. It does not come equipped to solve math problems beyond its capabilities. It does not come equipped
to prophesize and know for certain that this love will last
or that this enthusiasm will prove a meaning opportunity,
even though it is supposed to say—and mean—exactly
such things at the altar and on job applications.

We must understand that we are evolved and not
designed. With that understanding comes a huge sigh of
relief as we suddenly realize that we are bound to manifest shortfalls and that we will regularly dismay and disappoint ourselves. It also brings an equally huge warning
sign as we recognize that neither we nor the rest of our
species are adequately equipped to handle personal, com-
munal, or species-wide challenges.

This warning is twofold. We remind ourselves that
we must be alert to the many challenges that we will have
to meet with respect to this experimental brain. We also
remind ourselves that our fellow human beings are not
who we would like them to be but who they are, and that
we are going to be challenged by *their* brains. To take just

Why Smart People Hurt

one example that repeats itself throughout the history of our species—and that will continue to repeat itself until we are different creatures—we will have to deal with those of our fellow creatures who have become either authoritarian leaders or authoritarian followers.

Theodor Adorno, the German-born sociologist associated with the phrase *the authoritarian personality*; Else Frenkel-Brunswik, a psychoanalyst and German émigré; and the UC Berkeley social psychologists Daniel Levinson and Nevitt Sanford championed investigations of the authoritarian personality back in the early 1950s. They took as their starting point the Freudian model of the psyche and argued that a certain sort of punitive, rigid, and conventional upbringing produced a child, and then an adult, forced to control his roiling id with a punitive and rigid superego. They argued that certain traits arose from this particular and precise dynamism, traits that coalesced into the authoritarian personality.

They concluded that the authoritarian personality comprised nine qualities or psychological orientations including anti-intellectualism, cynical destructiveness, a superstitious nature, and exaggerated concerns about sexual activity. Whether or not their model is accurate, the phenomenon can't be missed unless you close your eyes to it. We may not genuinely understand why authoritarian leaders and authoritarian followers come to be, but we are obliged not to act like we don't see them. They too are the fruit of this experimental model and are one of the ways that *our* brain is taxed as we try to fathom how to live in a world full of brains dreaming up ways to dumb us down, rule us in bed, and restrict our freedom.

We are the sort of creature who not only needs to put up firewood and food for the winter but who must also predict the distant future, make decisions about who or what created the universe and what sort of principles and path we should follow, deal with our fellow difficult and dangerous creatures, and in other ways make sense of things that would overtax any creature. It is easy to see how we might have evolved into exactly this situation—and then be stuck here. This amounts to a really terrible stuck place: imagine a machine that, grinding away at jobs too hard for it, progressively wears itself down and, possessing no off switch, never gets a moment's peace off the line.

If it is by thinking that we weave our picture of the world, speak to ourselves about what we need and what we want, and try to solve our personal problems, then it follows that we will turn to our brain and to the thing that it does—think—to meet these and every other pressing life challenge. We ask that it answer everything from whether we should buy this or that car to whether life is worth living. We ask it to solve problems, lift our spirits, and understand our life purposes. Naturally this taxes and stresses a brain that is only the experimental model and that, like everything else in the natural world, comes without a crystal ball.

Stress causes the greatest number of doctors' visits annually. Yet we haven't noticed well enough that the issue is not just what is stressing us but also how poorly we are built to deal with that stress. We ask our experimental brain to work overtime to decide what line will sell next season, whether our son is drinking just a lot or has become an alcoholic, whether this passing feeling means that the universe has a purpose or that our medication is kicking in, where we should look to heal the hole in our heart and make life feel worthwhile . . . and everything else.

Not knowing what else to do, we set our brain racing off, whether or not it has good brakes, whether or not it is equal to the task, and whether or not the task is reasonable. The smarter we are, the more likely we will use our brain in these ways, and the more painful pressure we are likely to produce. Just as you would expect a bull to have difficulty in a china shop should it get it into its head to purchase a nice dinner service for eight, so you would expect a human being to have trouble solving his problems with this precise brain—or with any brain that also generates awareness and consciousness.

It is a certain profound misunderstanding that causes part of the pain that a smart person experiences and one that can be rectified in an instant. You do not have a brain that was designed to work well in all circumstances and in all regards. It was not designed to be equal to its tasks or to magically have the power to predict the future. How much less guilty and upset you might feel if you understood this and accepted this!

A smart person ought to be smart enough to see clearly the limitations of his species. At the same time, he ought to roll up his sleeves and do whatever he can to deal with the peculiarities and shortfalls of this particular brain model. As charming as it is to speculate about what sort of brain we might have had or might one day have, for now our species has this one. Accept that and deal with the consequences as smartly as you can.

CHAPTER QUESTIONS

1. Given that we do not come with an on/off switch, what do you want to do when your brain races?

2. Given that our poorly calibrated early warning system produces a lot of unnecessary anxiety and even treats thinking as dangerous, what do you want to do when thinking makes you anxious?

3. If you picture yourself evolved rather than designed, what does that suggest about your species-specific strengths and weaknesses?

4. To what extent do you see above-average intelligence as a threat to a creature like you, and to what extent do you see it as a benefit?

5. Just for the fun of it, describe an upgraded or updated version of our species.

Why Smart People Hurt

5

THE LOGIC OF MANIA

This species that we currently are, this particular experimental model, has a brain of a certain sort with its particular capacities and tendencies. Countless metaphors have been created to capture aspects or qualities of this brain, from brain as spider web (delicate, minimal, and hypersensitive) to brain as lens (magnifying and intensifying energy to a profound point), from brain as lamp to brain as map, from brain as cookbook to brain as toolbox, and of course brain as computer, calculator, and so on.

For the purposes of this chapter, let's consider it as a high-performance engine in some of its aspects, capacities, and tendencies. It is an unusual and unique engine that we rev up but that also revs itself up and functions on its own, perpetually and for its own reasons. We can send it racing after a calculation and make it do math or balance our checkbook. But it can also send itself racing to create a dream or a nightmare, an obsession or a mania. In this regard, it is also something like a high-strung stallion that we can ride if we are masterful and careful but that can also gallop off on its own.

What are the features of this high-performance engine or high-strung stallion that cause smart people so much distress? One is that mysterious and potentially dangerous state known as mania. Mania can hit anyone—it can be induced by street drugs and by other causes, including the dynamics of one's own racing, needy brain. But here we'll focus on how mania arises from a person's reliance on brain activity to solve her problems, including her existential ones, and the special way that such reliance afflicts smart people.

People who think a lot are more prone to mania than people who do not think a lot. That intelligent, creative, and thoughtful people are the ones more regularly afflicted by mania is beyond question. Research shows a clear linkage between achieving top grades or scoring high on tests and suffering from bipolar disorder (that is, that so-called disorder in which depression and mania cyclically appear), and between other similar measures of mental accomplishment and a racing mind.

There is plenty of evidence to support the contention that mania disproportionately affects smart, creative, thoughtful people. One study involving seven hundred thousand adults and reported in the *British Journal of Psychiatry* indicated that former straight-A students were four times more likely to be diagnosed bipolar (or manic-depressive) than those who had achieved lower grades.

In another study, individuals who scored the highest on tests for mathematical reasoning were twelve times more prone to bipolar disorder. Similar studies underline the linkage between creativity and mania, and we have hundreds of years of anecdotal evidence to support the contention that smart and creative people often get manic.

The current naming system used to describe so-called mental disorders like manic-depression and bipolar disorder is weak and highly suspect, however. I've discussed this matter of the arbitrary, whole-cloth creation of mental disorders through certain ruses of definition, including the spurious defining of the term *mental disorder* itself, in *Rethinking Depression* and elsewhere. Here, let me just repeat a warning to be wary of employing or taking seriously the current mental-disorder naming system. In natural psychology, we completely eschew it.

The current naming system leads to odd and wrongheaded hypotheses, for example, that "because you are bipolar, you are creative" or that "perhaps mania accounts for the higher test scores." What is true is that the greater the reliance on thinking and the more brain capacity for thinking a person manifests, the greater his or her susceptibility toward a racing brain. If you are inclined to think, why would those thoughts *not* be inclined to race in certain circumstances?

If, for example, something threatened you or challenged you, why would your brain *not* race in its quest to deal with that threat or challenge?

What is called mania, in this regard, is simply a racing brain driven by a certain powerful pressure, need, or impulse. Anything that gets in the way of this seemingly forward motion—a physical obstacle, another person's viewpoint, even a delay in the bus arriving—is viewed as a tremendous irritation. Hence the irritability so often associated with mania. This irritation makes perfect sense: if you *must* get on with whatever your racing brain is proposing—get every wall painted red, capture that song, solve that theorem—*then nothing must get in the way.*

It is this *must* that is at the heart of the matter. The *must* is the foot on the pedal that is driving your racing brain. There is an emergency here, most often an existential emergency as the individual stares at nothingness and is petrified by the view. She must get away from that horrible feeling and, with a kind of strangled laugh that mimics mirth but isn't mirth, she turns to her brain for help. She is frightened and in anguish, and to deal with that, she shouts to her brain, "Get me out of here!" Her brain then takes off, dreaming up every manner of scheme, activity, or desire.

All of the characteristic symptoms that we see in mania—including seemingly high spirits, heightened sexual appetite, high arousal levels, high energy levels, sweating, pacing, sleeplessness and, at its severest, when the train has run off the rails, hallucinations, delusions of grandeur, suspiciousness, aggression, and wild, self-defeating plans and schemes—make perfect sense when viewed from the perspective that a powerful need has supercharged a brain already inclined to generate thoughts. This thought machine has been revved up in the service of nothing less than the direst existential hunger, lack, or fear imaginable. All the rest follows.

To switch metaphors, the stallion has been spooked and will crash through even the sturdiest fence in his wild, panicked flight.

The driving impulse may not be limited pain; it may not be pain at all. You may be working on a novel or a scientific theory that excites you and you can't wait to get on with it. Still, that excited pursuit, even though in pursuit of something positive and valuable, has caused your mind to move from a lower gear to a higher gear, dramatically revving up the engine that is your brain, and now that engine is whining and straining. A dangerous dynamic is now at play: are you driving the engine, or is the engine driving you?

Yes, you are still in the saddle and clutching the reins, but the powerful stallion may throw you at any second.

What can be done about this racing? Natural psychology has many answers having to do with the art and practice of making meaning. However, the short answer is increased self-awareness and the courage to see one's nature. It is the individual exposing this situation to himself and for himself, announcing that he must wrest control of his mind and his life, and practicing the techniques conventionally called mindfulness techniques, that amount to the short answer.

What we are actually talking about as a prospective solution or possible aid is not only conventional mindfulness, in which a person learns how to better deal with the contents of his or her mind, but a new awareness of the limits of thinking, the pressures of thinking on the organism, and the many other built-in challenges that come with having an experimental brain faced with outsized challenges. Let's call this new awareness *brain awareness* to distinguish it from mindfulness. The main tactic a person can use to deal with the problems flowing from having this particular experimental brain is brain awareness.

If a given individual won't do this work or at this split second can't do this work because her mania just can't be mediated by her own efforts in the state in which she finds herself, then she may indeed be forced to resort to the unfortunate conventional solution of psychiatric medicine. She may need lithium, anticonvulsants, calcium channel blockers, antipsychotics, benzodiazepines, or some other chemical used to supposedly treat mania and with the power (though only sometimes, and always with a physical and emotional cost) to do that work for her.

In the end, it is the brain-aware manic individual herself who ultimately must accomplish the odd and seemingly impossible task of saying, if only in a whisper, "I know that I've set my own brain racing, but that racing isn't really a very good answer; no, creating mania isn't the answer." Perhaps our next brain model will come with an off switch and we will be able to shut the machine down as wanted, but for now, the only off switch we have is smart inner conversation.

In natural psychology's view of what is going on, where it is completely understandable and plausible how this wild ride came to be, we ask the individual—demand of him if we love him—that he examine his reasons for racing and not feel so free to race. It is not a race that can be won, a truth the brain-aware manic knows somewhere in his being and a truth that brings with it additional sadness even at the height of the racing, as the manic races but knows that he can't outrace existential distress.

Indeed, it is that very sadness that the manic is fleeing as fast as she can, even as she is racing right toward it. It is like the Sufi tale of the disciple who flees his town because he believes that Death is coming for him there, and he races right to the place where Death is waiting. That is exactly where the manic also arrives—at depression.

Mania is completely understandable as a natural result of setting a brain racing in support of the huge tasks, like making meaning, that human beings face. If, for example, a creative person experiences creating as a meaning opportunity and is pressured to race in the service of her creative efforts, she may usually be able to mediate that mania. But sometimes that pressure may overwhelm her. There is no simple off switch that she can throw—which makes this risk all the more real and dangerous.

There is, however, an off switch that people *do* try to throw. They try to white-knuckle calmness. They don't really feel calm, but they do everything in their power to act calm and be calm—maybe using alcohol to help, maybe using mindfulness to help, maybe using constant activity to help. This is why we don't see more frankly manic people. Smart people everywhere are doing their best *not to be manic*, hanging on to the reins of their racing brain as one might hang on to the reins of a wild stallion.

This is exhausting work, and sometimes these people are unequal to it, just as one might be able to hold on to the reins of a wild stallion for a while but for only so long. At some point, that powerful animal rips the reins right out of a wrangler's hands. Nevertheless, smart people are for the most part built pretty well to hang on to calmness and to avoid full-blown mania—at the cost, however, of a tremendous amount of energy expended to maintain their white-knuckled calmness.

Even as they hang on, they are enticed by that mania. Consider the following analogy. If you live in a castle and pillagers periodically roar through your kingdom, bandits roam the countryside, and wild animals lurk in the under-brush, you know that you are safer inside the walls than outside. But what if you know or suspect that somewhere out there are psychedelic parties, wild river rides, strange never-before-seen sights, and all the excitement and meaning that is so patently lacking here in the castle?

The pressure is bound to mount and you rationalize that it is probably safe to go outside given how serene the countryside looks, how rarely bandit sightings and wild animal attacks are reported, and how wondrous the sights and sounds to be found out there are. The dangers aren't apparent and the payoffs feel enormous. Sooner or later, a person is going to get castle fever as he stands on the ramparts and gazes over that lovely landscape that looks so serene. He is bound to stare so hard that he will begin to see mirages of meaning out there.

Smart people tend not to realize the extent to which both their forced calmness and their mini-manic activities are more ways of defending themselves against letting their mind roar away in mania than affirmative lifestyle choices. They are unnaturally calm or constantly busy not so much because they love calmness or love keeping busy but because they do not want to permit the indulgence of mania. They are making an honorable effort to keep their racing mind in their own control—at the expense of what may prove to be unhappy lifestyle choices and huge expenditures of energy.

As a result, most smart people prevent themselves from launching into full-blown mania. They do something else instead: they so assiduously guard against this wild ride that they live becalmed, in a forced state of calm that is very much like a straightjacket. Many smart people are living a forced calm life so as to help themselves deal with what would prove a manic way of life if they dared to let themselves go. They intuitively know just how dangerous and powerful the engine of their mind is, and for safety reasons, they tread very carefully through life.

You would think that a person would need to experience full-blown mania at least once in his life in order to recognize it as something that he does not want to experience ever again. Nor is it that children watch cautionary videos about mania in school, as soldiers are made to watch cautionary videos about venereal disease, and are taught to avoid it. Nor does anyone around them warn them about it. So why is this threat perceived as so very dangerous when it is neither taught, talked about in casual conversation, or personally experienced?

The likely answer is that intimations of the dangers of mania come with the original endowment that makes a smart person who he is. He is probably built right from the start to be one of those people who recognizes himself in that crazy manic man on the street, who sees as part of his future the manic episodes of a Beethoven or a Byron, the one brushing aside waiting piano students because music is dying to come out, the other racing across Britain on a rampage of sexual encounters with married women and young boys. Somehow he knows that he has that in him—that knowledge is a feature of his original personality.

If you have been endowed by nature with a brain that can race, it makes some sense to suppose that you have also been born with intimations of the dangers of allowing that brain to race. And it may perhaps also be the case that some numbers of smart people are born *without* this built-in understanding of how dangerous mania can be—and therefore are less effective in protecting themselves against its onslaughts or actually invite it into their life. Just as a given person can look down at the edge of a thousand-foot drop and experience no vertigo when, one might guess, nature should have built her to back away, so a given smart person may be built without a sufficient sense of the dangers of full-blown mania.

A smart person therefore faces two different but related threats, the threat of painful, white-knuckled calmness that feels like self-created boredom and a prison sentence, and the threat of uncontrolled mania that is painful in the experiencing and that is likely to culminate in despair as she realizes that her manic efforts did not change the facts of her existence. Forced calmness or uncontrolled mania? Of course, neither is the right answer—and we will provide a best possible answer when, in our final chapters, we paint a picture of how the principles and practices of natural psychology can help.

CHAPTER QUESTIONS

1. Do you experience mania?

2. How does it express itself?

3. Do you feel that you keep yourself artificially calm as a way of dealing with incipient mania?

4. To what extent can you let your brain race but still remain in control of it?

5. To what extent are you at once attracted to mania and frightened of mania?

6

FEATURES OF A RACING BRAIN

According to a Princeton National Health and Wellness Survey, 37 percent of US adults reported insomnia or sleep difficulties during a recent twelve-month period. Between 40 and 60 percent of people over the age of sixty suffer from insomnia. Two million children suffer from sleep disorders. More than 10 million people in America use sleep aid medication to deal with their insomnia. Fifty-five percent of all adults report having problems with insomnia in their lifetime. More than 70 million Americans suffer from various sleeping disorders, and 60 percent of those 70 million report severe sleeping disorders.

What's going on here?

Exactly what we chatted about in the last chapter.

In large measure, what is going on is a simple, straightforward thing: our experimental brain has trouble quieting itself, even at the cost of a good night's sleep. It races on—even though we are in bed—broods about what went on today, and worries about tomorrow. Built without an off switch, it can't completely shut itself off, and one manifestation of that difficulty is insomnia.

Our brain has a job to do, to protect us, to serve us, to solve our problems and to make sense of life, and often it will continue to do that job irrespective of our wish to sleep. Our ability to think, the quality that distinguishes us from other creatures, may have evolved to protect us and to serve us, but as an unintended consequence, one that doesn't threaten our species but that plagues each smart individual, that very ability to think can keep us awake as we try to fall asleep, or it could force us awake once we've fallen asleep.

This is true for everyone, but it is especially true for smart people who possess a brain with more racing power than average. Every problem associated with a racing brain covered in the previous chapter and in this chapter is more of a problem for a smart person than for the next person for the simple reason that her brain is more powerful. If you put your foot down on the pedal of a car with a horsepower of 90, you won't produce the same speed and drama as you will if you floor a racecar. A smart person employs her brain to solve her problems and to keep her safe, and by putting it into gear in her service, she starts a powerful engine racing.

Consider the following analogy. If you knew that a campfire would keep away a pack of nearby wolves, you would learn how to keep your campfire burning throughout the night so that you could get some sleep while keeping the wolves at bay. And what if in your sleep you heard wolves approaching or the campfire sputtering? You would wake up abruptly and check to make sure that the fire was still burning. If it were nearly out, you would rebuild it. You would pay attention to that camp-fire because your life depended on it. That is natural, sensible, and straightforward.

What if the threat isn't wolves but a risky investment, a chronic illness, an alcoholic child, an infuriating job, a difficult choice, a vexing problem, a treacherous mate, a depleted bank account, an edict against your group, a threat to your identity, a blow to your ego, or a meaning crisis? What then? Well, your brain will feel threatened and will deal with that threat in the only way it knows how: by thinking. It can't rebuild a fire or take a shot, for there is no physical action to engage in as you try to sleep. All your brain can do is keep working—that is, race.

Our brain broods, problem solves, calculates, obsesses, stews, and races in our service. It will do that day or night; it is indifferent to the fact that we might need our sleep. It is odd that we have failed to realize the extent to which our need to rely on our thinking in order to survive naturally produces insomnia. Your brain stews, it hatches plans, it rehashes its grievances, and all that stewing, hatching, and rehashing is likely to keep you awake, just as keeping an ear peeled for danger will disturb a cowboy's sleep.

We have reached a point as a culture when our first inclination is to label insomnia as a *disorder in need of treatment* and head in the direction of doctors, sleep clinics, medication, therapists, space-age technology, and similar help. Natural psychology suggests that you look in the mirror first and see what sort of creature you are, what sorts of perils a creature like you regularly encounters, and the extent to which you are bound to employ your brain to deal with those perils.

Insomnia may prove a terrible affliction, but it is not strange. It is exactly the sort of thing that you'd expect to afflict a creature with a brain that races. If you are indeed being kept awake by your own racing brain, it should be clear that you are obliged to learn how to reduce your brain's racing if you are to get a good night's sleep. Applying brain awareness to the situation—that is, understanding that you are this kind of creature and learning tactics and techniques that can quiet a racing mind—is the closest you can come to possessing the off switch that nature has failed to provide.

There are organic, biological, and medical reasons for some cases of insomnia, and you want the appropriate medical treatment if the root cause of your insomnia demands that sort of attention. But before you seek medication, which may be prescribed to you irrespective of the actual cause of your insomnia, it makes sense to wonder if perhaps you are having trouble sleeping because your brain is racing. In most cases, that will prove the source of your troubles and suggest in which direction you should look for relief—that is, toward some form of mindfulness.

Techniques like mindfulness designed to quiet the mind ought to help with insomnia and may well help more than medication can. Yet in our medicate-first culture, this contention needs saying and proving. It is therefore excellent that studies like those run by Cynthia Gross and her colleagues at the University of Minnesota, which showed that after eight weeks of mindfulness training, participants who learned mindfulness fell asleep more quickly than the medication group—and had the benefits last over time—are run and reported.

You will sleep better if there are no wolves prowling your wilderness; that is, you will sleep better if you are not actually threatened. Would you expect to sleep better during a bombing raid or once the war has ended? Would you expect to sleep better during a financial crisis or after the crisis has passed? Would you expect to sleep better if your mate is abusive and a threat to you or if he no longer lives under the same roof? Threats matter, they are real, they are dangerous, and they set our mind racing.

Mindfulness techniques are extremely valuable, but equally important is threat reduction. You can meditate for an hour every morning, but if when your husband comes home, he criticizes you and then ignores you, your meditation practice probably won't prove enough to get you a good night's sleep. A divorce may be needed. If you experience your profession as meaningless, your meditation practice will probably prove insufficient. You will also need to change your life so that you feel less threatened, less sad, less anxious, less rageful, less upset with life, less self-reproachful, and so on. Then you will sleep better.

We have evolved with a brain that is supposed to handle difficult tasks—everything from fathoming family secrets to mastering calculus to maintaining meaning to counteracting shortfalls in our own formed personality—as well as outright impossible tasks, like predicting whether a profession is appropriate based on zero real knowledge of that profession and only a current enthusiasm. A smart person is even more likely to suppose that his brain is equal to the challenges he faces, even such frankly impossible ones. What a setup to send your brain racing! And what will it do when, racing, it realizes the magnitude of its challenges and the extent to which they can't be solved just by thinking? It will worry.

Rather than actually think about anything, it will start worrying.

Given that this brain of ours is confronted by difficult and frankly impossible tasks that it presumes it should be able to handle, having not gotten the message that it is evolved and not designed and that it is only an experimental model, at some point it will start to think less and worry more. It will worry in ways that produce sacrifices to the gods, runs on banks, and unfinished novels. It will worry in ways that produce superstitions, mental confusion, and cognitive distortions. Sensing the dangerousness of the world and its own limitations, it will spin like a top with worry.

It will worry—and have a Scotch, and then another.

It will worry, not being able to picture how ten tons of steel can fly, and refuse to ever take to the air.

It will worry, fearing that it is already hapless and ruined, and sink into sadness.

It will worry, certain that it can control nothing, and spend all day controlling its environment by organizing socks.

When such a brain tries to think, its worries will interrupt its thinking, just as a wild stallion will stop its galloping to sniff the air for danger. It tries to think clearly about its current situation, and after a minute, worries intrude. As a result, it thinks poorly, which convinces it all over again that it can't think well enough to handle its challenges. Might the next version of our brain worry less? Or would that make it too vulnerable to dangers? This model, at any rate, is wonderful at worrying.

How does this worrying manifest itself in a smart person's life? Here is one among countless examples, as reported by Claudia:

> One of my challenges is rooted in two simple words: what if? I pester myself with those words constantly. A couple of decades ago, a therapist, visiting me at my home because agoraphobia kept me from going to her, told me to try to stop asking, What if?, all the time. I wasn't even aware I was doing it! Once she warned me to stop, I saw that I was doing it all the time.
>
> This is how it works. Let's say I get an invitation to go somewhere fun (for work or pleasure). Instead of just saying yes and moving on, I enter into a barrage of thoughts like: *Is there parking close to the entrance? I hope it's on the first floor. Can I figure out how to go alone in case I change my mind? Is there a way to go other than that road with the cattle chute lanes? It better be air-conditioned.*
>
> After much online searching about every aspect of the experience, should I say yes to the invitation, I go through a period of confidence that I can successfully go. Then, as the

event nears, although I look like I am present in the real world, I am actually living half in another place where I am what if-ing in my head all the threats to my agoraphobic limitations and scheming myriad ways to get out of the commitment.

I don't share this with anyone; I internalize it and basically drive myself nuts. The only time I can get the thoughts to stop is when I get lost in something very creative and puzzle-like—and then I only get lost briefly. This way of life is exhausting and keeps me from living and from reaching my full potential. I wish I weren't still in this place, but I can't get my brain to stop its self-pestering.

The results of this predictable dynamic, that a racing brain sent off in pursuit of answers that aren't available will start attacking itself instead—results like pestering obsessions, soothing compulsions, addictions and quasi-addictions, phobias, reckless counter-phobias (like sky-diving to deal with a fear of heights), anxieties, and so on—are distressing and natural, not a disease or abnormal. That as a smart person, whose brain races faster and harder than the next person's, you can't accomplish something like stopping your racing mind from worrying doesn't mean that you have a disorder or that you are a failure. Rather, it means that you are a product of imperfect nature and that nature has sent you a special challenge that may prove extremely difficult to meet.

It may require remedies and interventions that you would prefer not to contemplate. It may require that you spend real time every day using available techniques to reduce your experience of worry. In some cases, it may require chemical interventions, not because you have an illness but because chemicals produce effects and you may desperately want those effects. What it absolutely requires is that you practice brain awareness: that you understand what this particular brain model can and can't do and how it characteristically runs amok.

One unfortunate answer that smart people often employ is to settle on some rigid way of being that seems to serve them and that simplifies their thinking tasks. In effect, they let their formed personality trump their available personality. This way of being is natural and biologically economical but shrinks them and prevents them from making value-based meaning, since the activity of making meaning requires daily flexibility and daily intention. They become something—the steely prosecutor, the cynical reporter, the spiritual artist, the busy mother, the lifelong predator—and respond in rote and repetitive ways to save themselves the hard work of actually living.

What if the way you use your brain as a prosecutor isn't the appropriate way to use it when you sit down to have a chat with your son or when you go out on a first date? If it has become second nature for you to always prosecute, if that is the way your brain works when it is on autopilot, and if you are unaware or unconcerned that this pattern makes everyone you meet feel threatened and uncomfortable, you're likely to find yourself without friends, family, or loved ones. That is a high price to pay for not realizing—or not caring—that your way of handling this experimental model of a brain is to lock it into one gear.

A smart person is likely half-aware of all of this—and finds it rather humiliating. He started out with a good feeling about his brain; he likely felt smart from the beginning. For those first few moments at least, the world was his oyster. Then he experienced life and learned about life, including the life of his own brain. Out of the box, its cracks, blemishes, and shortfalls became obvious. How sad! And how humiliating.

Slavoj Zizek explained in *How to Read Lacan:*

> Freud developed the idea of three successive humiliations of man, the three 'narcissistic illnesses,' as he called them. First, Copernicus demonstrated that the Earth turns around the Sun and thus deprived us, humans, of the central place in the universe. Then, Darwin demonstrated our origin from blind evolution, thereby depriving us of the privileged place among living beings. Finally, when Freud himself rendered visible the predominant role of the unconscious in psychic processes, it became clear that our ego is not even a master in his own house. Today, a hundred years later, a more extreme picture is emerging. The latest scientific breakthroughs seem to add a whole series of further humiliations to the narcissistic image of man. Our mind itself is merely a computing machine

for data-processing, our sense of freedom and autonomy is merely the user's illusion of this machine.

This is a lovely summary of our current situation. These further humiliations are rooted not so much in the fact that our brain is merely a computing machine but rather that, as splendid and intricate as it may be, we are exactly what we are: this current model of human being. We are not who we might have been or who we would like to be. We are exactly who we are. This truth leads to a further painful humiliation, one that I've dubbed "the smart gap," and that is the subject of our next chapter.

CHAPTER QUESTIONS

1. What do you see as the challenges associated with a racing brain?

2. Given that as a species we do not possess an off switch to turn our racing brain off, what tactics and strategies might you employ to keep your brain from racing when you don't want it to race?

3. If you are troubled by insomnia and see it as a racing-brain problem, what might you try to quiet or control your brain so that you can sleep more peacefully?

4. What will you do when answers to the problems you are trying to solve aren't currently available to you and your brain starts racing in search of those unavailable answers?

5. What ineffective tactics have you used to deal with racing-brain problems? What might prove more effective?

Why Smart People Hurt

7

THE SMART GAP

It is a poignant feature of our species that we can contemplate intellectual work that we can't quite accomplish. Forgetting for a second all of the difficulties associated with the construct of IQ, a person in possession of an IQ of 160 is not a better person than someone who possesses an IQ of 120, but she is better equipped to do abstract math. However, she herself is less equipped than someone with an IQ of 180, and that person is less equipped than a person with an IQ of 200. That is all natural.

It is also natural that we will experience emotional pain when we recognize that the work we would love to do—whether it is physics at the highest level, constitutional law at the highest level, psychological fiction at the highest level, or biological research at the highest level—is, if not completely unavailable to us, just unavailable *enough* to make it doubtful that we can proceed and just unavailable *enough* to make our efforts feel like torture.

In such circumstances, not only may you not be able to proceed with the work you deem most meaningful to you, but you will also know that you are not moving forward because your brain needs just *this much* more horsepower. As a result of this knowledge, you may decide that life is a cheat, blame your upbringing for robbing you of some measure of your native intelligence, and in other powerful ways experience sadness and frustration—all because of a naturally occurring gap between what you want or need and what you have.

This is an emotional pain that psychology hasn't examined: the pain of wanting to do certain intellectual work but not being equipped enough to do it. It's easy to empathize with the pain of a minor league ballplayer who is *just not quite* good enough to make it to the big leagues. Indeed, excellent documentaries have been made following the plight of exactly such players. We watch such documentaries, and we understand.

We've seen documentaries about dancers who aren't quite able to rise to the top because they lack some physical endowment. We've seen similar documentaries about pianists, about violinists, about singers—that is, about professionals in fields where we can *see* this natural diversity. But what would there be to see if we followed five mathematicians? Since there would be nothing to see, this problem has no public face and little power to provoke a public discussion.

In part because these challenges are invisible, we tend not to think about them or talk about them. But they remain painfully real for the people who suffer. It is in the American psyche to act as if there is an answer to every problem, but what happy face can we put on this particular problem? That short stout man, while he may make the occasional beautiful shot from mid-court, really can't play center for the Celtics. That singer with an ordinary voice really can't compete for the lead in *Tosca*. Some things are genuinely a matter of endowment.

You may not be fast enough for your ambitions, tall enough for your ambitions, beautiful enough for your ambitions . . . or smart enough for your ambitions. There is no good answer to this problem. But there are tactics available to reduce the emotional pain produced by this problem as well as tactics to make meaning despite the meaning crisis that a problem of this sort produces. We'll look at those in a moment.

This smart gap is experienced in all sorts of poignant ways. Janet, a writer, explained:

> When working on fiction, particularly when writing narrative in the third person, I can "hear" quite clearly the tone of the prose that I'm trying to capture. I hear this tone in my head much as one hears a piece of music in a silent room. But all too often, the prose that I write falls far short of what I'm hearing. It's like I'm playing a sonata on a long-neglected piano. The text doesn't ring true to my ear— it comes out in the extremes of sounding either glib or overdrawn.
>
> Despite my years of experience as a professional editor, I can have great difficulty getting the words on the page into the same key as what I hear in my head. Applying the usual technical improvements doesn't help;

in whatever way the writing falls short, it's far more mysterious and ephemeral than anything addressed in Strunk and White or *The Chicago Manual of Style*. When I'm not able to get it right, I end up feeling that I don't have the chops to live up to my own artistic vision as a writer.

Is this precisely a smart gap or something else? It could certainly be something else. Maybe this author simply needs to write more and worry less. Maybe her problem is a lack of experience and a lack of that accumulated wisdom that comes from putting in tens of thousands of hours at something. Maybe her environment is too noisy; maybe her mind is too noisy. Maybe she is burdened by too many responsibilities and cares. But it may also *be* a smart gap problem—and if it is, that will hurt.

Consider the following plaintive report from a teenager I'll call Fernando and two friendly responses to Fernando's commentary. Fernando wrote:

This is exactly where I have found myself over the past twelve months or so. I am seventeen years old. I graduated one and a half years early from high school and was expected to enter college as soon as possible (I have assumed that I would go to college for as long as I can remember). But I became obsessed with the fact that we have innate abilities and that I would never be able to reach any greatly significant level in the field of biology where I hoped to study.

So instead I don't do anything and find myself loaded with antidepressants. If you look at any given field as a tower, there are those who are content on the lower stories or content simply to methodically climb as high as they can climb; and then there are those few people who will get to the top. I fall into a third category: those who may make it very high but are destined to look up sorrowfully at the top that they will never reach because they simply don't have the abilities. I have always been prone to depression and obsessive-compulsive disorder, but there is such logic in my sorrow that I can't seem to pull myself out of this hole.

Emily responded:

Fernando, you are very self-aware. I suspect that very awareness is relevant to your depression and your obsessive-compulsive disorder. But I also think that you've turned up the heat with a fear of failure and kicked away the ladder of possibilities, killing off any escape from your frustrating dilemma. Success in any field is the result of multiple factors. Intrinsic talent is a bonus to any pursuit, lessening the struggle to competency or mastery, but it doesn't necessarily predict success.

Individual motivation can be a powerful force behind hard work, persistence, and other variables and can compensate for lagging talent and natural disadvantages. Maybe there will always be some individuals who surpass your accomplishments, your talent, or your intelligence, but that doesn't mean that you can't pursue your interests, your dreams, and your life. Your contributions could be unique and highly valued, and your participation could put your life onto a path to something amazing.

Don't give up on yourself. Living with mediocrity may be abhorrent to you, but with the help and support of friends and family, with professional advice and guidance, and with more life experiences, you'll learn to cope. Trying is better than living with regrets. It's easy for me to say, but don't be afraid of failure or mediocrity—they can be sage teachers and can help you overcome adversity.

Roberta offered the following:

Fernando, I agree that a smart gap can sometimes exist, but I can't ignore my internal revulsion at the fatalistic overtones of such an idea. I also agree that people should be somehow well matched to their endeavors, but if that were always obvious at the beginning, many greats would not have pursued their paths and many current celebrities would certainly not be famous!

Why not think about the following steps that may help you achieve what you're after?

1. Choose your life's work according to your interests, passions, and ability.

2. Learn the history of your field and current trends in your field.

3. Practice, practice, practice.

4. Work with masters in your field.

5. Surround yourself with others who share your interests.

6. Learn the written and unwritten rules of your profession and follow them.

7. Accept that mastery takes a long time to achieve.

8. Experiment, innovate, and find your personal style.

9. Understand what your audience, your customers, or your employers want and supply it.

10. Monitor the results of your efforts and make changes as necessary.

I agree we are not all Einstein, but Einstein is an icon to be admired, not a blueprint for individual success. IQ and talent are two pieces of the puzzle, but they are separate from achievement, which requires a high amount of effort, adaptation, and strategizing to produce the external rewards we seek. Manifesting worldly success through innate ability is a complex combination of efforts.

Emily and Roberta's responses to Fernando's predicament are very reasonable. They are practical, optimistic, and clear-eyed in their understanding that accomplishment and success do not necessarily or even usually relate to a person's pure brainpower. Intellectuals and intellectual lightweights have become president. Intellectuals and intellectual lightweights have written bestselling books. Therefore it is certainly the case that you do not want to write yourself off too quickly! If you sense that a given thinking line of work is a potential meaning opportunity, you don't want to dismiss it—especially because any given individual's menu of meaning opportunities may prove short rather than long.

At the same time, smart gaps do exist. They exist for all of us. To some extent, we can narrow the gap; to some extent, we can ignore the gap; to some extent, we can work around the gap; to some extent, we can reconcile ourselves to the gap. Making meaning entails exactly such efforts! But if on a daily basis you want to make meaning in a certain way and you can't because of some shortfall in your native capacity, that is going to hurt, and that is going to matter.

If such a gap exists for you, it is good to be honest and clear about its existence and to then think through what you want to try to do to bridge it, if that is possible, or otherwise deal with it if bridging it isn't possible. It is a worse policy to deny the existence of a gap you are experiencing, even as it causes you distress and even as it affects your ability to do the work you've set out to do, than to forthrightly acknowledge the gap—and then strategize.

What can you do?

First, you can help your brain be its best. This means many things, from not drinking alcoholically to silencing negative self-talk that robs you of confidence to tackling your chosen intellectual subject in a regular, disciplined way. It means deciding to get a grip on your mind, think fewer small thoughts for the sake of your big thoughts, distract yourself less, flee from the work less, and make fewer excuses about why you don't have the time, patience, or ability to think.

Second, you can contemplate what intellectual work matches your native ability. It is entirely possible that devising the most complicated plot in the history of plotting serves you considerably less well than choosing a simple plot that allows you to write a deep, lovely, but also straightforward novel. Maybe there is a puzzle in your field that suits your brainpower, a corner of your field that is delicious and also not too hard, a way to do the work you want to do that makes use of your other strengths. You will only know if any of this is possible if you admit that there is a problem, step back, and consider your options.

Third, you will want to be kinder to yourself. How many smart people torture themselves to the point of institutionalization over the fact that they can't turn out poetry as brilliant as the poetry produced by their idols, can't solve a mathematical problem that has thwarted all the biggest brains, or can't create summations like Clarence Darrow? You can torture yourself and threaten your mental health, or you can decide that such self-torture hardly serves you and strive to stop it.

Fourth, you might make your primary intellectual work matter a little less by making multiple meaning investments and seizing multiple meaning opportunities. That is, rather than putting all your identity investments, intellectual investments, ego investments, and meaning investments in, say, your biological research, you might invest in it and also in activism, in service, in relationships, in enjoyment, in just being, or in other areas likely to provoke the psychological experience of meaning.

Fifth, you might surrender to the possibility that you don't really know one way or the other whether the smart gap you sense is a real biological impediment or a function of something that might change with time and effort.

You might in a sense dismiss its reality, act as if it didn't exist, and see if it narrows or vanishes as you work hard at your chosen discipline. You acknowledge the gap, thumb your nose at it, go about your meaning-making work, and monitor if the gap was perhaps a chimera all along, if it's perhaps narrowing, if it remains wide but no longer seems that important, or if it remains a pressing issue.

In this last instance, if the gap remains real and significant, if it continues to matter to you, and if it feels unbridgeable, you can redouble your efforts by working to update your personality, quiet your mind, increase your knowledge base, or with some other tactic. Intelligence is not fixed. We are smarter on some days and duller on other days. We sometimes get excellent ideas several steps above our intellectual pay grade. You can certainly build a little optimism into your considerations about whether you are smart enough for the work you want to do. Tempered by that optimism, however, must be the clear-eyed understanding that we have not been built for the purpose of solving puzzles that are too puzzling for us.

These gaps amount to real problems in the lives of smart people. Whether the gaps are bridgeable or unbridgeable, more real or more imagined—whatever their exact nature or their exact reality in a given situation—when you sense a smart gap in an area of life that matters to you, it is bound to produce the experience of pain. Reducing that pain is essential. You might try different tactics of the sort outlined in this chapter and others I'll chat about at length in future chapters. But it is imperative that you do something. Living in pain while trying nothing is not the answer.

CHAPTER QUESTIONS

1. To what extent have you experienced the smart gap described in this chapter?

2. Does it affect you only in certain areas of thinking and not in others? Are there areas of thinking where you are perfectly smart enough and other areas where you are poignantly not quite smart enough?

3. What tactics might you employ to see if this smart gap is real or alternately a function of some problem, like acute anxiety, that might be solved or corrected?

4. In what sense, if any, might you make yourself smarter?

5. If this smart gap turns out to prove an intractable problem, how might you work around it?

Why Smart People Hurt

8

THINKING ANXIETY

People who perform tasks known to provoke anxiety are obliged to deal effectively with that anxiety if they want to perform that task well. Dancers, singers, actors, and other performers have to deal with performance anxiety. People who must fly for a living—including pilots and flight crews—have to deal with their fear of flying if that fear afflicts them. And people who think for a living or who regularly employ their brain must deal with the real, undeniable, and often severe anxiety of thinking.

Even if we are essentially equal to a given thinking task and even if there is no disturbing smart gap to contend with, smart people will still have to deal with thinking anxiety—that is, with the anxiety that arises in us as we try to think. Just imagine getting caught in an elevator trapped between floors. Thinking often feels exactly like that. Trapped in the confined space of our own brain with a test question, a work-related issue, a personal problem, a research challenge, or an artistic conundrum that's pressuring us into an answer, our anxiety mounts.

Every manner of thinking, from calculating to imagining to predicting, produces a certain amount of natural anxiety that might be handled relatively easily once we acquire some simple anxiety management techniques to deal with it. Our usual way, however, is to not see the anxiety coming and to have no good plan for dealing with it, to be surprised anew each time, and to employ one of the following seven unfortunate anxiety reduction methods. Therefore, smart people, who have to deal with this anxiety more than the next person, need to be especially alert about moderating their use of, or not employing, the following common but unfortunate tactics.

We Flee the Encounter

To avoid the anxiety that we half-know is coming, we do not go near thinking, we veer off in another direction as we approach a thinking task, we begin to think and almost immediately get up and do something else, or we stay put but send our mind somewhere, somewhere easier on the system. Very often, we just shy away from thinking altogether. Like the person who is afraid of flying and steers clear of airports, a person made anxious by thinking may simply steer clear of it.

Maybe we manage to begin to think but experience the anxiety mount as the answer to the test question or the direction to take with our research continues to elude us. At some point, we stop thinking about the problem itself and only notice our distress and our desire to end the distress. Our mental confusion caused by the anxiety worsens, we are less able to think than when we first sat down, and we know it. Maybe we jump up; maybe we distract ourselves and forgive ourselves with thoughts like: *I can do this tomorrow,* or *I need to do more research,* or *Nobody gets every question right.* Maybe we stay put, tortured and not thinking at all, until our workday ends or the test examiner tells us to put our pen down.

How rarely do we actually make it to the end of a chain of thought in good order? We flee before we start thinking, we flee it as soon as we start thinking, we flee some tortured minutes or quarter-hours into the thinking, we flee via fantasy, we flee via distraction, or we check our email or play "just one" game of computer solitaire—we find fifty ways to leave our anxiety. Perhaps worst of all, we may talk ourselves right out of our belief in the project we've been tackling. To ease the anxiety that comes with thinking, we announce that the novel we're writing isn't working or that our scientific theory doesn't hold water. We drain meaning right out of the enterprise so then we can leave—righteously but despairingly.

We Use Dangerous Canalizing Tactics

In order to make ourselves stay put as thinking anxiety wells up in us, we scratch at our head, maybe until it bleeds, we bite our fingernails, maybe until they are bitten down, we keep a Scotch bottle handy, or in some other way soothe ourselves as we struggle to think.

Picture a canal filled with rushing water. You are in charge of this water but not in control of it. It is your precious charge, but you can't control how fast it rushes through the canal and, unless you take measures, you are threatened with losing some portion of this precious water sloshing up over banks. This is important, tension-producing, and even exhausting work, and while you are engaged in this momentous struggle, you may not notice that you've been clenching your jaw, chain-smoking cigarettes, or scratching your head raw.

This image of a canal filled with turbulently rushing water may help you better understand the phenomenon of canalization of energy—that is, the efforts we make and the habits we adopt to keep our thoughts on track and in the canal as they rush along. Many of these tactics produce no large negative consequences—our finger-tapping may do little more than annoy our neighbors in the café. But if your method is smoking cigarettes, you risk lung cancer. If your method is scratching at your scalp, you risk bleeding sores. If your method is clenching your jaw, you risk jaw injury.

How difficult will it be to quit smoking if you are using smoking to canalize energy and reduce anxiety as you think? It is one thing to deal with the addictive power of nicotine and another, maybe even harder task, to try to quit when smoking has become your number-one anxiety management technique. And what if your repertoire of canalizing techniques includes cigarettes, alcohol, and another drug or two? Can you see a poly-addictive problem looming on the horizon?

We Think Small

We may have a certain novel in mind that we want to write. We sit down to begin it, anxiety quickly wells up in us, and we decide to write a blog post instead. Writing the blog post allows us to congratulate ourselves on having gotten something done—but inevitably those congratulations will be mixed with feelings of disappointment and chagrin since we know exactly what our real intention was when we sat down.

A given architect may dream of *really* thinking about his next steps as an architect but feel anxious each time he entertains the thought only to discover that he has spent two decades profitably but boringly engaged with remodels. Each day he goes through the motions, working hard, solving countless practical and tactical challenges, making money, feeding his family, and taking care of his obligations. No one could fault this picture—except, as is so often the case, the architect himself, who wanted more from a life in architecture and who recognizes that some large thinking about architecture never occurred just because of anxiety.

Small may be beautiful, but it is less beautiful if we meant to do something larger and especially if we know that it is only the larger projects and the larger challenges that provoke in us the psychological experience of meaning. In that case, small is not beautiful but an incipient meaning crisis. Thinking anxiety can cause what at first glance seems like an unthinkable outcome: preventing us from experiencing life as meaningful. If we meant to work large but we shrink from that task because of anxiety and work small, we may find the consequences of that self-soothing maneuver dramatically negative.

We Think Safe

It is much easier on the brain for it to be asked to repeat a memorized message than to think. Most people who regularly communicate with others do not think on their feet, as that is hard and anxiety-provoking work, but instead craft a message and then repeat it. Those repeated messages are woven into their stump speech or become the tapes that they run. We sound more intelligent and more confident and do a better job of staying on point when we just repeat our messages.

When our boss stands up, he speaks automatically. When the principal at our daughter's school stands up, she speaks automatically. When an author is interviewed about his latest book, he speaks automatically. Indeed, this is expected and demanded, since folks who are engaged in public performance have almost zero permission to gather their thoughts, take their time, and think on their feet. Our modern world has eliminated pauses.

It is natural that we will do the same sort of thing internally to reduce or eliminate the experience of thinking anxiety. Instead of actually thinking, we run a tape, tell ourselves a story, dredge up an old thought, return to a comfy place in our mind, and play it safe. Folks run their tapes in public, and they also run their tapes internally. They will find ways of rationalizing why they seem not to be having any good new ideas and may even create a rationale for the benefits of avoiding good new ideas. That rationale then becomes the tape they run, further soothing them.

We Fantasize

As soon as thinking anxiety begins to mount, a smart person—someone who naturally loves story, metaphor, narrative, and fantasy—may, for example, stop working on his novel and instead fantasize about winning the Nobel Prize. He purposefully lets his mind wander and fantasize success, conquests, revenge, or anything else that might prove soothing and distracting. Some of the time, the daydreaming quality of the thinking person is a state of working reverie in which his mind wanders in the service of his thinking tasks; more often it is simple, soothing daydreaming.

Because the brain of a smart person is so agile with narrative, it can spin itself lovely fantasies all day long, winning a battle with ferocious creatures in the morning, winning at love at midday, and winning a Pulitzer in the evening. Good brains regularly do this. But fantasizing doesn't get diseases cured, novels written, children bathed, or homes built. Those vicarious exploits are not real exploits, and in the end, a person fails to make himself proud by succeeding only in his daydreams.

In the language of natural psychology, you garner the psychological experience of meaning—and make yourself proud in the bargain—by making value-based meaning investments and actively seizing meaning opportunities that present themselves, not by spinning fairy tales. Overindulging in fantasy is a regular risk for people endowed with the ability to create beautiful narrative who know that if they were to stop fantasizing and turn to their thinking work, along would come anxiety.

We Overprepare Ourselves

There are countless prethinking activities—from research-ing to list making to brainstorming to brain quieting to informational interviewing to workshop attending to file organizing—that may serve our thinking needs but may also be dodges that we use to avoid our actual thinking tasks and their attendant anxiety. Often these are varia-tions on the theme of "I can't begin until I am absolutely ready." Is a person who says that a lot typically ever ready?

It is absolutely the case that we may not be able to solve the problem in theoretical physics that we've undertaken to solve unless we attend a certain confer-ence where we stumble upon a missing piece of the puzzle or read a journal article that provokes an insight that leads us to a solution. But it is also the case that if we are not actually working on our problem, if we are only say-ing that we are working on it when in fact we rarely think about it, then it is altogether likely that we will sit in on that lecture or read that journal article and gain nothing.

The activities meant to help our thinking only help our thinking if we are thinking. If, because thinking makes us so anxious that we secretly avoid it, we engage in potentially useful activities only for the sake of mak-ing a good appearance, maintaining our identity, and soothing our nerves, those activities are unlikely to prove particularly useful. In a corner of awareness, we probably know exactly the game we are playing—which further distresses us and disappoints us.

We Try to Circumvent the Process

Thinking is a process that, like all genuine processes, comes with unavoidable mistakes and unpleasant messes. Because these mistakes and messes are quite real and produce negative consequences—like sending our novel off in the wrong direction and taking two years to recover from our misadventure—the thinking process naturally produces pain. Who wouldn't want to circumvent or skip all that?

It is part of the process of thinking to add two plus two plus two plus two and, because we are tired, distracted, or momentarily dumb, get ten, which error perhaps only causes us to misunderstand how many people are showing up for dinner and buy a little too much salmon or which error causes us to incorrectly set our sights and fire on our own troops. Thinking is a process that comes with errors. That very thought provokes anxiety! To repeat, who wouldn't want to circumvent or skip all that?

But you can't. Thinking is that sort of process. You will be led down false paths and drawn along by false scents. Your best guesses will sometimes prove completely in error. The facts at your disposal may be wrong. You may have a good hour and undo that good thinking with a bad minute. That is what is. We may wish that it were different, we may find ourselves attracted to seminars called things like "The Ten Tricks for Mistake-Free Thinking" or "The Secret to Perfect Thinking," but what we are actually doing is avoiding the process, avoiding the anxiety, and avoiding doing the thinking.

John, a biological researcher, explained:

> I use all these methods! I had no idea I was
> doing any such thing until I encountered this
> list. I had no idea that my cigarette smok-
> ing, my procrastinating, my fantasizing, my
> reading yet another journal article, and my
> opting for a tiny corner of my field when in
> fact my heart is interested in much larger
> questions are all connected at this base level
> as ways to avoid the anxiety of thinking or
> to deal with it when it commences. Now I
> see exactly how they connect! I have to face
> the fact that aiming my brain at a difficult
> research question and tackling that question
> is going to make me anxious—period. I have
> to embrace that truth . . . and deal with it!

Imagine that you run marathons. That is a hard
thing in and of itself, yet most marathoners stick it out
and manage to cross the finish line. The essential hardness of the enterprise doesn't prevent them from com-
pleting their task. But imagine that running a marathon
was more like thinking. Now you would face the added
challenges of not being certain which turn to take, not
understanding the route markings, not being able to see
the road in the intermittent fog—and, as a result of these
new difficulties, growing anxious. This makes for a much
harder marathon! At some point, these added difficulties
might even make you throw in the towel.

Thinking is like running a marathon in a thick fog with our anxiety mounting. One of our jobs, if we are to cross the finish line, is to deal effectively with that mounting anxiety. We do this by actually learning how to effectively manage anxiety. There are scores of techniques to try—breathing techniques, cognitive techniques, relaxation techniques, stress discharge techniques, reorienting techniques, disidentification and detachment techniques, and more—all of which amount to nothing if an anxious thinker won't try them. We'll return to this theme when, in a later chapter, we examine the smart practices you'll want to adopt to deal with the many challenges we've been discussing.

CHAPTER QUESTIONS

1. Does the act of thinking provoke anxiety in you? If so, how does that anxiety manifest itself (that is, what are its symptoms)?

2. What tactics (like fleeing the encounter, smoking cigarettes, keeping your thinking small, etc.) do you use to soothe yourself and reduce your experience of thinking anxiety?

3. What would you like to try instead in order to reduce your experience of thinking anxiety?

4. Describe your plan for staying put with your thinking, even if thinking makes you anxious.

5. If this is a serious problem for you, what additional steps do you want to take in order to deal with the anxiety of thinking?

Why Smart People Hurt

9

THE LURE OF LANGUAGE AND LOGIC

Abstract words do not have simple meanings or straightforward uses. From their complex and confusing richness arise all sorts of demands, seductions, lures, and traps.

Philosophers, social scientists, cultural observers, linguists, politicians, advertisers, and anyone else with an interest in what influences people know that nothing, not even so-to-speak real events, has as much power over people as does the language that human beings contrive to use.

George Orwell wrote in "Politics and the English Language":

> Political language has to consist largely of euphemism, question-begging and sheer cloudy vagueness. Defenseless villages are bombarded from the air, the inhabitants driven out into the countryside, the cattle machine-gunned, the huts set on fire with incendiary bullets: this is called pacification.

Millions of peasants are robbed of their farms and sent trudging along the roads with no more than they can carry: this is called transfer of population or rectification of frontiers. People are imprisoned for years without trial, or shot in the back of the neck or sent to die of scurvy in Arctic lumber camps: this is called elimination of unreliable elements. Such phraseology is needed if one wants to name things without calling up mental pictures of them.

Smart people are likely to harbor the sense that they routinely see through the common tricks played on them by those who use language to tyrannize, persuade, or sell. They know to smile wryly at another "new and improved" or "buy two, get one free." They shake their heads when clerics, politicians, and economists speak. They understand the game being played by television talking heads, where fiery debate is just another ratings ploy. Smart people are likely to feel far above the ubiquitous fray of language manipulation . . . but of course they aren't.

Not only are smart people not immune to this power, but they are doubly influenced by it. Just as everyone else does, they find themselves ensnared by the metaphors produced by their society, by their media, and by their ruling classes. Even though in a corner of awareness they may know better, they end up as manipulated and coerced as anyone else. On top of that, they create their own ensnaring metaphors with the power to hold them in sway even for a lifetime.

Their very smartness, which causes them to love language, to find language pregnant with meaning, and to use it as their primary organizing tool, inclines them in the direction of turning language into existential handcuffs. How does this work? It works in extremely simple and straightforward ways. A young boy reads a book about the missing link and ends up with a PhD in archaeology and a lifelong attraction to Africa. Even if at some point he finds the idea of a missing link passé, unnecessary, or wrongheaded, and even if he no longer sees himself on that particular quest, he has nevertheless organized his whole life around a pregnant phrase that somehow *meant so much to him* when he first encountered it.

For a budding Einstein, the ensnaring phrase might be *unified field theory*. For a budding writer, the seductive string of words might be *great American novel*. The snare need not be a phrase—it can be a single word. For one smart person it might be *painting;* for another it might be *cosmology;* for a third it might be *justice.* Words and phrases of this sort are like magnets that organize the iron filings of our feelings, beliefs, needs, and values into powerful demands and elusive holy grails.

These words and phrases are experienced as powerful meaning opportunities, as *the* place to make meaning, and as such can trump all other considerations, including those that really ought to be considered. Yes, *accounting* may not possess the meaning charge of *performance artist* but when, because of the power of language to ensnare, we lose our chance to even think about whether some profession or way of life might actually serve us, we severely limit our real possibilities.

Words like *novel* or *spirit* are bundles of meaning that, like bundled kindling, ignite into blazing fires in the imagination. How beautiful, brilliant, and dangerous they are! To what extreme places can a word like *novel* or *spirit* take a person! The novelist may remain poor forever, the monk may remain silent and celibate forever, all for the sake of what a word is signifying in her imagination. It is time that we understood the tremendous extent to which all people, and smart people in their special ways, find their lives both illuminated and constrained by the power of language to create the psychological experience of meaning.

What should a smart person do about the power of language to affect him like this? There is no simple answer and worse, no really good answer. If you stick a pin in every word and consciously drain it of its power to affect you and of its ability to hold meaning, you have effectively reduced your chances of experiencing meaning and dwindled your actual experiences of meaning. You are wiser, yes, but also sadder. To take the magic, mystery, and potency out of words like *painting, cosmology,* and *justice* is to make life smaller and duller. Is that what's wanted?

On the other hand, if you never deflate the puffed-up words and phrases that you are using as your life's organizing metaphors, then you will find yourself caught in their snares, led around by the nose by them. You will experience powerful negative consequences if, as so often happens, their reality is not equal to their resonance. If, in pursuit of the truth, beauty, and goodness generated by the word *justice*, you become a death penalty lawyer and in thirty years of practice grow exhausted as you save not one single person from execution, how well has the power of the word *justice* served you?

Because natural psychology identifies meaning first as a subjective psychological experience, second as a certain sort of idea, and third as a certain sort of evaluation, we have a way to think about this profound dilemma. Using the ideas and language of natural psychology, the death penalty lawyer in question might say to herself: "I am getting no psychological experience of meaning from my death penalty work, even though I still love the word *justice*. I don't want to pull the plug on that word, but I must completely reevaluate to what extent I want to organize my life around that metaphoric word as opposed to organizing my life in some other way. What should I do next in the realm of meaning, and how should I hold the word *justice* next?"

It isn't that a painter must stop being a painter or that a cosmologist must stop being a cosmologist just because she sees to what extent the words *painting* or *cosmology* have lured her and ensnared her. Rather, she must step out of the snare and examine her situation with fresh eyes to see whether she wants to reinvest meaning in painting or cosmology or whether she wants to seize some other meaning opportunity, realizing that her next meaning opportunity, rooted as it is in language, may itself mesmerize her, mislead her, and ensnare her.

You are obliged to see through language, so as not to be fooled by its seductive power too badly or too often. You are also obliged to embrace language's magnetic resonance, or else life will feel gray and listless. However language came to be, it came with these two properties built right into it: that with it we create meaning and that with it we create lures and traps. One word can provide us with meaning for a lifetime; one word can enslave us for a lifetime. And yes, it might be the very same word.

The exact same issues stand when it comes to logic. Smart people love logic, but logic, and especially the semblance of logic, can also prove to be a lure and a trap. Logic and semblances of logic can create justifications for any position—including positions that a smart person himself does not support or believe in. It is tremendously easy to spin out a string of logical-sounding premises and conclude that it is immoral to eat meat or that it is essential to eat meat, that it is necessary to travel to Mars or that it is ridiculous to travel to Mars, that it is imperative to sign this peace treaty or that it is vital to wage this war, and so on. Smart people know exactly how to do this.

It is very easy to learn how to use semblances of logic to justify yourself. You begin a sentence with "I was taught that . . ." and end with an argument from authority. You counter a request with "You want me to take out the garbage, but you won't have sex?" using the logic of symmetry to disguise your refusal and your complaint. You use causality to make your points: "The school shooting wouldn't have happened if (guns weren't so easy to obtain) (they didn't teach evolution in the schools) (teachers were better paid) (parents did a better job of disciplining their children)." A smart person can get good at this and win arguments by ending them as soon as they begin.

Why Smart People Hurt

Certainly, some smart people have the patience or the desire to examine arguments to see if they are sound and solid—to see, for example, if the argument's premises already include its conclusions or whether terms and phrases have been used clearly and consistently. However, not many people, smart or otherwise, have the time or the energy needed to analyze the arguments foisted on them wherever they turn. Consequently, in a world of light logic and talking points, no smart person has all that much trouble arguing his case—irrespective of the truth of the matter and irrespective of his own beliefs.

Why is this important? Let's consider just one example. Freud was brilliant at moving from a thought, for instance that some dreams are perhaps interesting in revealing what a person is thinking and feeling, to grand conclusions like the dictum that "dreams are the royal road to the unconscious." He used language and semblances of logic to create a profession where none existed and did such a beautiful job of sounding right that, a hundred years later, people are still recounting their dreams to paid professionals and engaging in what they presume is a helpful process that will reduce their emotional distress.

It is very alluring to use language and logic in such ways, to feed our ego and our everyday narcissism by creating whole fields or even gods out of whole cloth, and to stand preening alongside our creations. The ease of this and its alluring nature leads to, among other serious problems, whole generations of bullies, some as smart as the original thinker and some not so smart, who from their master's hand possess resonant metaphors and serviceable scripts that allow them to look professional and earn a living.

If, for example, you are a client in therapy with a certain sort of analyst and have the audacity to want to chat about something that did not appear to you in a dream, the analyst simply will not allow it. This may strike you as farfetched, and yet it occurs all the time. Here, for instance, is a report from one such client, as reported by the analyst Louis Breger in *Psychotherapy: Lives Intersecting*. The client reported:

> In my first session, this psychologist prompted, 'Did you have a dream?' I did. She listened attentively and then offered some interpretation. When I told her that the interpretation didn't really resonate, she explained that this was due to my resistance. This irritated me. She indicated that my irritation was an indication that her interpretation had touched a nerve, and that we were, therefore, on the right track. The sessions were always the same—I would begin by talking about events in my life—she would listen impatiently and eventually interrupt me with, "Did you have a dream?"

It is terribly easy for a smart person to use language and light logic to leap to conclusions that serve her— emotionally, egoistically, professionally, or in some other way—and to then stand behind them in an authoritarian, unrelenting, bullying way. It is terribly easy, for example, to take constructs from science, romanticize them, and turn them into spiritual and occult metaphors that their theoretical reality doesn't support. The special combination of alluring language and light logic can come together and, without any justification, can turn scientific speculation into proof of the existence of gods.

As a smart person, you can make believe that you have landed on an incontrovertible truth just by stringing words together in a certain way. If, for example, you say that this partakes of that, then you have created two things just by saying so. By snapping your fingers, you've simultaneously created and proven dualism. All you have to say, for example, is that chocolate ice cream, in order to *be* chocolate ice cream, in order to have that real ontological chocolate ice cream-ness, must necessarily partake of an essence of chocolate ice cream-ness, which means that essence of chocolate ice cream-ness really must exist, which in turn must mean that there are other dimensions in which the platonic idea of chocolate ice cream and vanilla ice cream and strawberry ice cream hover without melting.

There is nothing easier than creating a permanently refrigerated ice cream heaven.

You may be smiling while reading this, but in the history of human affairs, this is no smiling matter. These machinations and manipulations become the intellectual structure upon which everything from totalitarian governments to the psychiatric labeling and then imprisoning of dissidents to witch hunts and inquisitions hang. It is one thing to create an astral plane for ice cream flavors and another to create gods to whom you must swear allegiance. Here, for example, is Bishop Berkeley's proof of the existence of God as described in his *Principles*, #29:

> Whatever power I may have over my own thoughts, I find the ideas actually perceived by Sense have not a like dependence on my will. When in broad daylight I open my eyes, it is not in my power to choose whether I shall see or no, or to determine what particular objects shall present themselves to my view; and so likewise as to the hearing and other senses; the ideas imprinted on them are not creatures of my will. There is therefore some other Will or Spirit that produces them.

Ipso facto: God. No actual gods existed at the beginning of that paragraph and no actual gods existed at the end of that paragraph, and yet somewhere in those words, the existence of a god got proven. Any smart person can do this. Any smart person can use alluring language and light logic to explain why he should be paid more than someone else, about why his theory is more correct than another person's, and so on. I can do this; you can do this; all smart people can do this.

Maybe you understand this and are careful not to use alluring language and light logic inauthentically. The following challenge and its attendant pain will still remain. If you are aware of this dynamic, then you will see evidence of it all around you, and that is bound to make you angry. What if you see right through the latest, hottest pedagogical tool brought to your school by a well-known speaker? You can't begin booing and also keep your job. What if you get only mishandled logic from your fellow jurors? You can't run to the judge. What if the talking points of your town fathers are such thinly disguised power grabs that they make you want to scream? Will you embark on the heavy lifting of multiple recall petitions?

There may be virtually nothing you can do or literally nothing you can do in such situations. There you will stand, enraged, mocked by circumstance, and in pain. At the same time, you will be sorely tempted to use language and logic in exactly these same ways. Like every smart person, you will feel moved to use language and logic to defend yourself, make your points, and serve your interests. Therefore, you will have your own hypocrisy to deal with. These are the multiple horns of the dilemma that arises because our brain runs imperfectly on language and logic.

We'll continue this discussion in the next chapter as we examine the lures of fantasy and mysticism. For now, let me summarize. Our brain works in a certain way. It employs that fantastic and amazing thing: language—and language is a multi-edged sword. It comprehends logic—and can torture it and manipulate it. Many brain seductions and traumas occur by virtue of these twin talents. We may be seduced into a lifetime of work that barely interests us. We may be seduced into creating theories that rest on air—and then feel obliged to defend them. For a smart person, language and logic are miracles—and monsters.

CHAPTER QUESTIONS

1. In what important and perhaps even life-altering ways have you been lured by language?

2. What pieces of language still have the power to grab you in ways that you wish they wouldn't?

3. What pieces of language still have the power to grab you in ways that you are perfectly happy to live with?

4. Describe in your own words how logic can prove a problem.

5. Have you experienced such problems with logic and, if you have, what would you like to do if they arise again?

Why Smart People Hurt

10

THE LURE OF MYSTICISM

A smart person, one who perhaps had her mind filled with religious ideas as a child but who recognizes that genuine mysteries exist with respect to the origins of the universe, can experience real pain if she opts for an easy mysticism. By the same token, if she refuses to opt for that easy mysticism and announces that she doesn't know ultimate answers and can't know ultimate answers, then she falls prey to the coldness and sadness that come with suspecting that the universe is taking no interest in her.

Pain is waiting for her in either case, whether she tries to maintain a mysticism that she can see right through *or* if she sheds that easy mysticism but then doesn't know how to handle the resultant meaninglessness. As it happens, natural psychology provides a complete, satisfying, and uplifting response to this conundrum, one based on the idea of living the paradigm shift from seeking meaning to making meaning.

If, however, she happens not to land on this good idea, she can spend a lifetime mired simultaneously in both unhappy camps, drawn to one mystical or spiritual enthusiasm after another—one year a Catholic, then a Buddhist, then a pagan, then a Taoist, then something with no name but with New Age trappings, and so on— while at the same time paralyzed by the thought that the universe has no meaning. She is at once an unhappy seeker who is burdened by an uncomfortable truth—a truth that could be transformed into something motivational and comforting if only she knew the conversion process.

Here is a beautiful report that will stand as our single example of the arduous journey from an easy mysticism to an acceptance of genuine mystery and the tasks a smart person faces in making value-based meaning. Jennifer explained:

> My husband and I were both raised in fun-
> damentalist Christian homes and commu-
> nities. We attended a private bible college,
> where I was the full-ride presidential scholar
> for my class and we both held leadership
> positions. My husband became a youth pas-
> tor after his graduation, and we were mar-
> ried as soon as I graduated. I was barely
> twenty-one and a pastor's wife. The church
> was a fairly large one, and the youth group
> numbered around three hundred senior
> high students. We took these kids on trips
> and retreats nationally and internationally.
> For a Christian couple, we were everything
> respectable, attractive, and vibrant.

Last August around this time, we began researching some of those questions Christians often seek to avoid. After about six months of wrestling with the tar baby of doubt, we had to admit that we were atheists. This was quite a shock to us, and we did seriously consider living a lie and continuing with the ministry. Leaving was just so daunting. However, our sense of integrity simply couldn't handle such a life. So, in January we came out as atheists and sacrificed everything. Our entire lives were based on Christianity—family, friends, financial security, and worldview. We were shunned and berated, slandered and condescendingly pitied, all by people who had claimed to love and support us only weeks before. It was more agonizing than we had anticipated. I suppose our ignorance gave us courage, and I now appreciate our naïveté.

At the time, it was relatively easy to go on with our imaginations full of our epic martyrdom. We had a solid sense of the strength and veracity we possessed, even when most of those we had known and loved became spiteful and cold. Yet, the months wore on, the excitement died down, and loneliness grew up in its place. By spring, we were exhausted. My husband was listless and empty, and I was filled with a directionless anger. With the loss of our worldview, we had sacrificed the only way we knew of creating meaning. Our immediate families and a few friends had chosen to stick by us, but there was still a gaping void.

This would have been a perfect time for us to discover natural psychology. Instead, we muddled along for a while in near despair. At some point, we decided that enough was enough and that we needed to regain our internal locus of control by actively participating in our own story. We had been attending a local atheist meet-up group, and I began to lead a secondary discussion group for them. While reading on the Internet, I came across a woman who had recently escaped the cult-like movement, and I reached out to her and began helping her with the writing process of a book. We didn't yet possess the vocabulary of natural psychology, but what was beginning to happen was that my husband and I had started making new meaning investments.

At this point in the story, my husband began a conversation with a man attending our atheist group for the first time. He was comfortable in his atheism but still attended church and was an active member of the community there. He invited us to meet his wife so that the two of them could hear our story in greater depth. We gladly went and learned

Why Smart People Hurt

that his wife was paralyzed with fear at the idea of losing the internal and external comforts of Christianity. Because of this anxiety, she balked at the prospect of seeking answers to questions that she didn't want to ask. This cognitive dissonance was agonizing to watch and seemed unbearable for her.

It was at this point, looking for resources that might help her find some peace and comfort, that I encountered *Natural Psychology: The New Psychology of Meaning*. Before giving it to her, I read it myself. It was a great encouragement to me and inspired me to keep doing what I had already begun and more. I still fall victim to the idea that an action must have lasting, broad significance to be meaningful— likely a remnant of my theistic perspective.

One of the new ways that I help remind myself that I can invest meaning right here, right now is by painting. For example, I painted a canvas I dubbed *January Waning* in honor of the waning moon that presided over the first phase of our public apostasy. I made meaning by creating that painting, and the painting maintains meaning in what it says to me in an ongoing way about the end of our old lives and the beginning of our new lives of promise.

In this new life, I create meaning through acts of encouragement and support for others who are leaving their religion or struggling with the social issues of atheism. When my new friend was feeling guilty about "forcing" us to sit with her as she cried on a Friday night rather than going out and having fun, I told her that there was no place I would rather be. It was true. I explained to her that part of our ability to stabilize and thrive was exactly what we were doing at their house—creating meaning through the support and encouragement of others who are experiencing what we went through. And I again explained the idea of a meaning investment.

I can still taste the lingering shadows of meaninglessness, anger, and sadness that hang about the edges of my mind. Yet, they are no longer dominant. I hadn't even realized the progress I had made until this new friend, tearful and terrified, cried, "I wish I was more like you!" To be envied rather than pitied is quite a unique thing to hear from a Christian these days. She is right, though: I don't want her double life and her internal struggles. There is great freedom in choosing integrity over the veneer of acquiescence. I could have been a pastor's wife still, with abundant praise and respect from friends, family, and community as well as with the

financial security it provided. I would sacri-
fice it all again. My husband and I have nom-
inated ourselves as the heroes of our lives,
and I am content.

If you believe in a religion or if you enjoy spiritual
enthusiasms, then Jennifer's journey may not strike you as
worth emulating. You may well disagree with natural psychology's contention that human beings are not privy to
ultimate answers. What I hope you'll consider, however,
is the following: the extent to which natural psychology
actually *honors* mystery. Your choice isn't between mysticism and nothingness. Rather, it is the choice between
mysticism and genuine mystery.

It's a common prejudice that a naturalistic worldview, one based on the ideas of science and empiricism
and a rejection of the lures of language and fantasy, ruins
life's mysteriousness. The following is one typical expression of how a naturalistic worldview is bound to rob life
of mystery. Sam Keen, writing about the contributions to
philosophy of the theologian Gabriel Marcel, explained
in *Gabriel Marcel: Makers of Contemporary Theology*:

> For Marcel, the results of a naturalistic way
> of thinking are disastrous for human dignity.
> As the capacity to love, to admire, and to
> hope dries up, the functional man loses the
> ability, and even the desire, to transcend
> his situation of alienation and captivity.
> His world loses its mysterious character, it
> becomes "purely natural," and all things are

explained by reference to the categories of cause and effect. With the eclipse of mystery goes the atrophy of the sense of wonder. One may perhaps question and investigate a purely natural and functionalized world, but one may not stand in admiring awe with a sense of gratitude before a mechanism that will one day be completely understood.

Well, but it will never be understood, nor can it be understood. That is a completely ungrounded fear—if, in fact, that *is* the fear . . .

Man, in this view, is incapable of looking around him and acknowledging without wincing or worse, without falling down in despair, that he doesn't know anything about ultimate reality. In this view, man is simply too small for such acknowledgments. He fears that he might stop hoping or caring if he learned that the universe was perhaps indifferent to him. Could he feel gratitude for his existence or awe in the face of a starry sky if he suspected that he was neither designed nor loved? He thinks not. Therefore he opts for mysticism.

Built into this rationale for mysticism is the idea that man would fall apart if he acknowledged that life was just this: *just this* translating as "empty, cold, impersonal, and purposeless." But that isn't the right acknowledgment. The choices aren't between a false but soothing mysticism and an acceptance of an indifferent universe. Rather, the choice is between an easy mysticism and genuine mystery. This is a very different choice! It is one that a smart person can embrace and applaud—and even grow excited about. He never again has to bang his head against the brick wall of mystery. He can just let it *be* mysterious.

The mystic has made a poor choice, one that a smart person with a mystical bent will never really feel completely comfortable embracing. The mystic, instead of acknowledging that she has absolutely no clue as to what created the universe or how the universe operates, prefers to act like she understands—and, more than that, that the answer is simple and straightforward. If she has a scientific bent, she turns metaphors from physics into proofs of the existence of gods or of a cosmic consciousness. If she has no scientific bent, she simply opts for whatever occult system or language she is born into or that speaks to her.

Natural psychology, on the other hand, lets mystery be genuinely mysterious and not transparent, simple, or obvious. It never says, "It's all a great mystery, but really it isn't. Here's the answer in my latest DVD." It never anthropomorphizes the universe and says, "The universe wants this," or "The universe demands that." When it calls a mystery unsolvable, it means it. We're sure to learn more about the material universe. We'll learn more about how the brain operates, how matter works, and what fills up empty space. But even if we evolve into a smarter, wiser species in possession of a truckload of new scientific knowledge, we will still have no access to ultimate answers.

When a smart person finally admits that some mysteries can't be solved, she can relax and rejoice. When you honor what you know to be true, that nobody knows the ultimate answers, that there is a difference between what is not yet known and what can't be known, that guesses don't really count, and that easy answers like sitting on a mat or walking in nature may soothe you but answer nothing, then you can leave mysticism behind. Then you are ready for *the* answer: that you are obliged to take charge of the project of your life.

If she could tolerate the truth that the mysteries of the universe are unsolvable, the chronic mystic could get on with her life. A smart person can opt to accept that truth, sleep better, and rest easier, and feel no diminishment in her sense of dignity. Why should she lose her sense of dignity because certain questions can't be answered? What else does dignity mean but actively living by your principles and your purposes whatever life throws at you? A smart person can say, "I accept the reality of mystery; now, let me decide how I will live."

Natural psychology asserts that you will experience less emotional distress and twist yourself into fewer knots if you engage in value-based meaning-making and stand up in a dignified way for your values and your principles, come what the universe may. Human dignity has always been about, and will always be about, trying to do the next right thing in the real world that we inhabit. This is hard and confusing work, but it is no mystery why we undertake it. If we don't, we create our own distress and we fail ourselves.

CHAPTER QUESTIONS

1. Do you simultaneously hold a naturalistic worldview and a mystical worldview? To what extent are they compatible?

2. If mysticism has created problems for you, how have those problems manifested themselves?

3. If you want to retain a mystical worldview, might you also simultaneously adopt the idea of value-based meaning-making?

4. Describe in your own words how mysticism can prove to be a lure (if you think it can).

5. If you would like to embrace mysticism less, how will you go about doing that?

11

A FIRM BUT NOT PROUD CONVICTION

E ven if they happen to have succumbed to the lures
of language, logic, or mysticism (and maybe because
they've succumbed), a great many smart people entertain
enthusiasms, hobbies, and interests; pursue an education and then a career; and so on and yet never land on
anything—a subject, a line of work, a life—that they feel
passionate about. Even their enthusiasms, hobbies, and
interests bore them in short order. Here is how Sandra
described her situation:

> At forty-nine, I find that I have not been able
> to sustain interest in anything really. Art in
> the broadest sense is the closest thing. I'm
> not even sure if I prefer making it or looking
> at it. At home, I have a collection of artwork
> that I have done over my lifetime including
> sculpture, prints, drawings, etc., and nothing
> looks like anything else. It seems like such a
> chore to try to discipline myself to investi-
> gate a subject or style more than once.

The problem is, something in me wants to have that discipline, wants to explore a subject from different perspectives and in different contexts. But I battle with myself, saying I've already done it and there are a million other things to take on. My habit is to buy all the supplies needed to do an activity, let's say for beading bracelets, make one or two pieces—and I'm done. It's out of my system. And then? Well, I'm currently enrolled in classes on culinary basics, the history of the blues, the philosophy of film, and creative writing—and I want to take photography classes, sewing lessons, and singing lessons. That says it all.

I recently did a one-year volunteer stint assisting a recreational therapist at an adult day care facility, and I enjoyed that quite a bit. But I don't care to pursue that. It's like I'm always searching for something that will stick. I enjoy doing things like wrapping presents, inventing logo designs and critiquing movies on Netflix. Over the last few years, I explored ceramics, leather crafting, embossing greeting cards, cake decorating, art restoration, and acting (I auditioned and got a call asking what my schedule was, but I didn't have enough time available to rehearse!).

I like it all, but nothing sticks. There's nothing that I'm specifically passionate about. But

I wish there was. I can't help but feel that if I concentrate on one activity, I will be missing out on another. Am I just greedy? Do I have the passion but not the focus? I envy artists who can explore their subjects in depth and over time. It feels like I will live my whole life trying to decide what I want to be when I grow up.

Sometimes it is primarily a person's job that he takes no interest in while the rest of his life retains at least some luster. Gina, for example, explained:

All my life I've been looking for meaningful work. I am fifty-three years old with college degrees and a broad work experience. Every time I work somewhere, after a short period, I am bored. The "work" I really love to do is raising my children, writing, painting, and other creative things. But my paid work has never held any interest for me.

Gina is lucky because, often enough, it is *all* of life that a person experiences as boring and lusterless. Nothing excites; nothing holds much meaning. This can be switched for that, and that for the next thing, all with a half-stifled yawn.

This state of affairs should remind you of Kafka's "hunger artist," that sad figure from existential literature who could fast so well that, as a circus attraction, he spent his time wasting away in front of amused customers willing to pay to see his slow demise. From his point of view, he had no skill; it was simply that no food interested him. When asked by his supervisor how he'd acquired the "admirable talent" for fasting, the following interchange occurred:

> "But you shouldn't admire it," said the hunger artist. "Well then, we don't admire it," said the supervisor, "but why shouldn't we admire it?" "Because I had to fast. I can't do anything else," said the hunger artist. "Just look at you," said the supervisor, "why can't you do anything else?" "Because," said the hunger artist, lifting his head a little and, with his lips pursed as if for a kiss, speaking right into the supervisor's ear so that he wouldn't miss anything, "because I couldn't find a food which I enjoyed. If had found that, believe me, I would not have made a spectacle of myself and would have eaten to my heart's content, like you and everyone else." Those were his last words, but in his failing eyes there was the firm, if no longer proud, conviction that he was continuing to fast.

Many smart people find themselves in this odd situation, firm but not proud in their conviction that there is nothing in life that genuinely interests them or that *can* genuinely interest them. They claim that they would dearly love it if something *did* passionately interest them, and yet their claim sounds just a little hollow, as hollow

Why Smart People Hurt

as the hunger artist's. Is it really the case that a person in decent health and in decent spirits wouldn't find ice cream, pizza, barbecued ribs, or *something* tasty—or is it rather that he is indeed in poor spirits and down on life in a special way such that his appetite has been ruined?

Whatever the precise reasons for this malaise, countless smart people find themselves in the position of Kafka's hunger artist, wasting away, in love with nothing, and convinced that at second glance all pursuits turn empty. Nothing seems able to provoke the psychological experience of meaning in them or for them. They read a novel—that was okay; now what? They plant roses—that was okay; now what? They learn carpentry—they make a few objects; now what? They take a class—that was interesting enough; now what? They start a business— the stress outweighs the rewards; on to the next thing.

A person who stands as a hobbyist in life, bereft of meaning, despairs. Yet there is some odd stubbornness to her plight, as if she is determined not to give up her worldview even if another one might come with meaning, just as addicts fiercely hold on to their addictions and will only pay lip service—or no service at all—to the idea of recovery and a life without their cigarettes, cocaine, or alcohol. Indeed, many smart people become attached to both—to a life empty of meaning and to an addiction. The stubbornness soothing the pain produced by a stubborn refusal to take a genuine stab at making meaning.

Consider the following report from Frank that ties several of these themes together. Frank explained:

After years of fruitless effort, I don't know if I am even capable of feeling truly passionate about a particular subject, work, or life. Maybe I'm just not one of those people. This is actually one of my greatest fears: a long life of making due with enthusiasms. I suspect that one of the main hurdles for me is that I don't believe in absolutes. So, while I will probably never believe otherwise, I need to figure out if I am using this perfectly reasonable core belief of mine as a defense mechanism to do nothing but pursue enthusiasms.

When I was a young man, athletics interested me deeply. In college, when I began studying existentialism and reading the Russians, Camus, Sartre, and Heidegger and then Derrida, Lacan, Hegel, and Foucault, well, it was all heady stuff, and I got lost in meaning and meaninglessness and my own intelligence. I worked extremely hard to push my mind and my consciousness and writing papers for me became the most difficult and the most important thing in my life.

For the ten years after college graduation, my life was consumed by my alcoholism and drug abuse. I was either hopelessly sad, or I was ecstatic. I was either jobless or, having convinced someone of my "genius," in charge of something I knew nothing about nor cared anything about. Did I reach out to others out of genuine interest in their lives and selves? Did I allow them to define their own meaning in my life and accept them or reject them based on my own self-awareness and self-acceptance? Rarely. More often than not, I used the people in my life to prove to myself I wasn't a monster.

I haven't had a drink in a dozen years. Without question, if I were to die today, my last contribution to the misty vapors of shared consciousness would be my pride in this, the greatest accomplishment of my life. The rewards of a committed, hard-fought effort in a twelve-step program are huge and real. Some of my decisions in sobriety have been just as stupid as those in addiction, and some of my mistakes just as egregious. But I also know myself better—although the core problem remains.

Where does that leave me? I am a husband and a father of two. I am a writer and a graphic designer, gainfully employed by an insurance company to create brochures for its clients on the subject of employee benefits. I have changed jobs eight times in thirteen years. I am overweight and on two medications for high blood pressure and two medications for either a major depressive disorder or bipolar II, since I haven't seemed to respond to all of the medications or talk therapy.

Over the years, I have taken hundreds of tests to find out what I already know about my emotions, intelligence, aptitudes, interests, strengths, grit, outlook, etc. What I already know is that I have hundreds of enthusiasms, and I could make a very successful life around many of them. Teach math? Of course! Create and build a foundation supporting the arts in elder care settings? Why not? Study spiders? What could be better? Write and design employee benefits brochures? It's a living! And so on.

Lately, I am trying something new. I am lowering the dosages on my brain meds with the goal of getting off them altogether to see if my non-medicated brain is really all that bad. I am trying to implement natural psychology in my life. Yes, I have had the experience of nothing really interesting me deeply. This is my reality, and it is terrible. But my hope is that one of the real rewards of the twelve-step program and natural psychology is the knowledge that the answer isn't "out there somewhere." The key is that I have the courage and the resources to change things for myself and to try to live life in a more meaningful way.

Why Smart People Hurt

How might a person who has not found anything to love or any place to invest meaning change his life so as to increase his chances of falling in love with *something* and really investing in something? Natural psychology has many tools and practices for making these changes, and I'll describe several of them in chapter 18. For now, let's take a preliminary look at what our smart hunger artist might try.

First, he might make a new or renewed effort to acknowledge the problem. It is one thing to act as if you have identified a problem—say, with alcohol—and a very different thing to really acknowledge the breadth and depth of a problem. This acknowledgment is a mixture of surrender, acceptance, and honesty well-known in recovery circles as a necessary component of the process. In this case, he might finally acknowledge that his approach to meaning has not worked and that a new approach deserves scrutiny. Natural psychology calls this new approach value-based meaning-making, and our hunger artist might actively investigate it.

Second, he might learn some new language and the implications of that new language. He might learn to talk about meaning investments and meaning opportunities and begin to grasp what those phrases signify about the exact nature and location of meaning. He would sit down and try to articulate his life purposes, name efforts that would make him proud, describe how he wants to represent himself in the world and how he wants to be, and in similar ways paint a picture for himself *of* himself as the hero of his own story and the only arbiter of meaning in the universe. As a result, to take one example of what this change would signify, he would never just take a class again. Rather, he would carefully think through to what extent that class might or might not serve his life purposes and might or might not amount to a meaning opportunity.

Third, he might recognize and acknowledge that there must be elements of his formed personality, and perhaps of his original personality as well, that have made meaning a real problem for him—and that therefore he is going to have to pay real attention to his own personality and make his available personality really *available* to him so as to retrain and upgrade himself. Like someone who has felt occasional joy but who has difficulty being roused to joy, he is obliged to realize that he has a constitutional difficulty in being roused to meaning and that it is directly on his shoulders to do that rousing.

In short, he will need to *stand up*. This standing up, whether conceptualized as an act of courage, a commitment, an acceptance of effort, or in some other way, is the key gesture in the process. As he nominates himself as the hero of his own story and as the only arbiter of his meaning in the universe, he slowly stands up. At the end of the process, he finds himself standing. This is a completely different gesture from kneeling, meditating, sinking into the sofa, or fasting in front of amused spectators. He may not know what *precisely* to do now that he is standing—but he knows for sure that he has risen.

Next, he might draw up a list of the values and principles that he suspects or believes he cares about, not so as to rank them, since values and principles can't be ranked, but rather to reawaken in him the sense that values and principles matter and that these are the ones that likely matter to him. To see words like *truth, beauty, goodness,* and *justice* in front of him on a list that he himself has generated may help remind him *why* he has gotten to his feet and *what* he intends to do next. Creating such a list is a significant step in the meaning-making process.

There are more practices to look at and much more to say about this meaning-recovery process. No doubt each hunger artist became a hunger artist in his own way. There is almost certainly no single path to a lifetime of acute meaninglessness. There are so many ways to kill off meaning: by not caring, by not committing, by not finding the courage, by not choosing, by not besting demons, by not standing up. But the recovery process for each hunger artist can look identical. It involves a powerful, plausible shift in paradigm, mental model, and attitude in the direction of personal meaning-making—and with that shift, an end to fasting.

CHAPTER QUESTIONS

1. Have you been plagued by the problem of nothing really interesting you?

2. Do things stop interesting you almost as soon as you begin them, even if you begin them with enthusiasm?

3. There might be many reasons for this. To what do you attribute this problem?

4. How might you change your vision of life or your relationship to life so its potential meaning opportunities often, or at least sometimes, deliver the experience of meaning?

5. If you have a stubborn conviction that nothing will ever really interest you, can you loosen your grip on that conviction?

12

UNREASONABLE SELF-PESTERING

In the previous chapter, we looked at that sad state of affairs, so common among so many, of a life lived without sufficient meaning. There are many reasons why this happens, the primary reason being that people do not know that they have to make meaning in order to have meaning. A secondary but profoundly important reason is that many people, and smart people first among them, mentally pester themselves all day long and as a result allow little room for meaning.

This pestering is not just of the negative self-talk variety. It is equally what at first glance can seem like a completely reasonable pestering, in which you pose one reasonable question after another and then feel obliged to answer each of your questions. Take the following fanciful example, which is over the top but really not very different from the way that many smart people operate.

You're shopping at the deli and happen upon a nice-looking package of pastrami. Your mouth starts to water. Your brain goes, *Oh, pastrami! Yummy!* Then your brain starts pestering you by supposedly reasonably evaluating the situation: *Is the pastrami fairly priced? Is it right to eat another creature? Is the meat overly processed? Is it healthy to eat pastrami? Are those the smartest calories to ingest, or should I spend them on fruits and nuts? Do I like corned beef better? How much protein have I already eaten today? Does this supermarket pay its workers a living wage?* And so on.

You might retort, "Those are all reasonable questions." Indeed, they are. In fact, a given person might have even more questions. And still, all this over pastrami! Wait until you get to the cheese aisle, where cholesterol pops into your head, or the candy aisle, where diabetes pops into your head. Each of these questions may be reasonable in its own right—indeed, each is—but is so much appraising really necessary with respect to each of life's choices?

If those are all reasonable questions to ask with respect to that package of pastrami, then wasn't that appraisal process, even if it felt like mad self-pestering and too much questioning by half, exactly reasonable? The question then becomes, Is a point reached, maybe very early on in the appraising process, when such a bevy of reasonable questions amounts to unreasonable living?

That appraisal process, so reasonable when looked at from one vantage point, may also amount to too much attention paid by half. What this means is that a reasonable thought is not exactly the same thing as a thought that serves you. In fact, there may be a world of difference between any given reasonable thought and a thought that serves you. Isn't it possible that it is the latter that we must get better at countenancing and supporting?

Of course, the goal isn't to become unreasonable. Nor is it to become impulsive: *Let me just grab that pastrami, darn it all!* Nor is it to act like such matters are small stuff that should not be sweated, since they may in fact be significantly large: it may really matter to you how a deli meat is processed or whether a supermarket's employees are paid fairly. Where does that leave you? If these are reasonable thoughts and also not insignificant thoughts and *also* thoughts that do not serve you, how should you proceed?

Before we answer that, let's look at a more self-attacking example, an instance of a characteristic blend of negative self-talk and very reasonable appraising. Say that what you encounter is not a nice-looking package of pastrami but your own reflection in the mirror. You could just say, "Hi, there!" and be done with it. You could wave and smile. But you could also wonder if your hairline is receding; if your jowls are growing; if you've passed your prime and it's all downhill from here; if you've lost your last chance at love, as old and ugly as you've grown; if, in short, this reflection isn't a warning, an indictment, and more. Some of those thoughts are perhaps quite reasonable: maybe it is good to be reminded that if you want love, you'd better get right on finding it. Or should a person just rush by all mirrors?

What criteria can a smart person use to judge if a thought is both reasonable and also in her own service? The starting point of such an upgraded appraisal process is the following: that she remind herself that a thought's reasonableness is not reason enough to countenance it. Its reasonableness is only one criterion. We want a Dwight Eisenhower to quickly grab the pastrami or quickly not grab the pastrami but in either case get on with planning D-Day. In those circumstances, we do not want him torturing himself or slowing himself down with perfectly reasonable thoughts about his relationship to pastrami. We want him to get on with his most significant meaning ventures.

This is natural psychology's answer: that a reasonable thought is not worth countenancing (and, if possible, not worth generating) if thinking it fails to serve your meaning intentions. You make value-based meaning by thinking thoughts and countenancing thoughts that serve your meaning-making efforts, not by thinking thoughts that are merely reasonable. When you see your reflection in the mirror, you can scrutinize that reflection and interrogate it with poignant and intense questions that are each reasonable, or you can move right on to your meaning-making efforts. The latter is the way you create more meaning and less distress.

People tend to half-realize this. They tend to half-realize that there is something about thinking many of their quite reasonable thoughts that isn't ultimately reasonable. All that reasonable questioning feels like self-pestering and a personal inquisition because, in a corner of their mind, they realize they're slowing themselves down and deflecting themselves from pursuing their most important intentions. They can sense that this self-torture, rooted in reasonableness, is not useful, not in their best interests, and not really necessary.

Still, it can prove *very* hard for a smart person to break with the idea that a reasonable thought need

Why Smart People Hurt

not—and frequently ought not—be countenanced, or better yet, not even generated. Even if you can convince him that he will experience less anxiety, less distress, and less wasted time and motion, and even if he agrees that his meaning-making efforts are impeded by thinking and dealing with all those putatively reasonable thoughts, he is likely to find it wildly difficult not to examine and take the temperature of every reasonable thought that his brain generates.

It can feel downright dangerous not to know if the pastrami has additives and downright immoral not to know if the supermarket is underpaying its employees. As our reasonable thoughts are so often connected to these two profound concerns, our safety and our ethics, it is hard to tell yourself, "Those quite reasonable thoughts aren't serving me." Maybe the picture to keep in mind is that of Dwight Eisenhower poring over a food label or performing an Internet search on supermarket practices instead of planning D-Day. If we have meaning to make—and we do—and if those meaning-making efforts are rooted in our values and principles, as natural psychology's mantra of making value-based meaning suggests, *then we need to get on with those efforts*.

There is room for a great deal of misunderstanding with regard to this point. You may still be thinking, *But a reasonable thought is, well,* reasonable. *How can it be wrong to think reasonable thoughts? And what would happen if people stopped thinking reasonable thoughts? Aren't people unreasonable enough already? Isn't this a slippery slope to stupidity and incivility? No, this just doesn't sound like a good idea!* Somehow that sounds, well, undeniably reasonable.

It will prove easy to misunderstand this point if you think that the choice is between thinking reasonable thoughts and mistrusting or denying reasonableness. Those aren't the choices. Rather the choice is between thinking a given reasonable thought and continuing to think scores of its brothers and sisters, so many of them that it amounts to self-pestering and even self-torture, versus getting on with the *more reasonable* task of making meaning. Every thought is a cost, and the cost of many of our reasonable thoughts may prove just too high.

It is actually a more reasonable reasonableness that you are opting for when you decide to think fewer reasonable thoughts about that pastrami, your reflection in the mirror, your painful past, or your chances for success—unless, of course, those precise thoughts are necessary to your meaning-making efforts—versus getting on with the *more reasonable* work of attending to your meaning-making efforts. There is a higher reasonableness to consider than the mere reasonableness of a given thought: the higher reasonableness of living life as you intend to live it.

Is there any evolutionary value to this particular reasonable self-pestering? Does it provide some sort of mating advantage because, to make a joke of it, a miserable demeanor is so sexy? No. Self-torture of this sort is not an evolutionary advantage but rather is an accident of evolution, an artifact of consciousness.

When you evolve a thinking creature, you evolve a creature that will think about all sorts of things, including its place in the universe (too low), its path (too hard), its accomplishments (too few), its hopes (too dashed), and its day (both too busy and too empty at the same time). It will think all sorts of things—including a bevy of unreasonable, reasonable thoughts.

A thinking creature that is not provided with an off switch or with a simple cognitive regulator will just think on, turning itself into more of a brooding machine than a thinking machine. If you want proof that we are not intelligently designed, just imagine designing a creature like us that keeps nipping at its own heels and tripping itself up by its own thoughts! If we are designed, it is by someone with much too much fondness for burlesque. In the end, all of that reasonable appraising becomes a kind of deep self-unfriendliness as we intermittently realize that we are spending too much of our life countenancing thousands of reasonable but unnecessary thoughts.

This species-wide self-unfriendly thinking is exacerbated in a smart person by her very ability to think better than average. Because she's smart, she's likely not only to chastise and sabotage herself but also to dream up clever self-assaults. She's likely to attack herself mercilessly and at the same time provide superb reasons why the attacks are justified. She can think; she can evaluate; she can debate; she can access her values and principles; she can turn a fleeting thought into a brilliant closing argument. What excellent tools to use against the self! And, because she is smart, she is the very person likely to believe that the reasonableness of her reasonable thoughts is *why* she should entertain them.

It is wonderful if a smart person can begin to see through the putative reasonableness of her many reasonable thoughts. If you have two hours at your disposal and it is important to you that you have a certain difficult conversation with your adolescent son, then it is not reasonable to spend that period doing some other pestering reasonable thing like weeding your garden, planning your menus for the week, catching up on the world news, or making sure that the storm windows are in good working order. You could make a case for any of those activities, but only abstractly and out of context. In context, they are of secondary importance and hence not really reasonable.

Nor is it reasonable in this context to *think about* weeding your garden, planning your menus for the week, catching up on the world news, or examining your storm windows. In this precise set of circumstances, those thoughts are all deflections, distractions, and elements of denial. You would be making meaning if you rehearsed what you wanted to say to your son and rehearsed your responses to his denials, explanations, and justifications. You would be making meaning if you researched some information on the Internet relevant to your son's situation. You would be making meaning if you practiced your anxiety management technique in anticipation of this stressful conversation. To think about the storm windows or the garden, no matter how reasonable your concerns about their state of repair are, is a contextual travesty.

A smart person's self-pestering can seem *so* reasonable and therefore somehow necessary and even inviolate. At the same time, he knows that he's pestering himself unnecessarily. It is amazingly beneficial to see this dynamic for what it is and to try to respond to even quite reasonable thoughts in a new way, with the following question in mind: does this thought serve my meaning intentions? If you do not set all thoughts, whether reasonable or unreasonable, true or false, negative or positive, against this core question, then you will provoke distress on two fronts. First, you will have to deal with the anxiety that you've managed to provoke by "reasonably" worrying about the storm windows, the garden, the pastrami, the news, and so on. Second, you will feel guilty knowing that you've secretly used these reasonable thoughts to soothe yourself and to avoid your more important meaning-making tasks.

If knowing where to invest meaning is a problem for you, if you don't really know what's important, valuable, or significant for you to pursue, then it will be that much harder for you to shelve these pestering reasonable thoughts. In an important sense, you don't really know how to answer the question, does this thought serve my meaning-making efforts? You are stuck not having a way to judge if a thought is worth your time if you haven't quite figured out what *is* worth your time.

Previously, we looked at tactics for determining how and where to make meaning, and we'll look at more tactics further on. Here, let me repeat the headline: getting a grip on your own mind is part of the process of stopping unreasonable self-pestering, but just as important is getting a grip on what is actually important to you. If you don't know what the big stuff is, it will naturally be that much more difficult not to sweat the small stuff. Small stuff looms large when the big stuff is unknown. If you currently don't know what's important to you, *please decide*.

The task is deciding.

A smart person has a brain that is likely to unreasonably pester her with one reasonable thought after another and continue to pester her at the expense of meaningful living. Hopefully, it will dawn on her that reasonableness is the not the only criterion for countenancing a thought. More important is whether or not the thought serves her meaning intentions. To ascertain that, she will need to decide what her meaning intentions are, at which point that woeful pestering may suddenly diminish. Can it miraculously cease altogether? No—reasonable thoughts are reasonable, and we must let some number of them pester us. But we can dramatically reduce their number if we keep our eye on meaning.

CHAPTER QUESTIONS

1. To make a small joke of it, do you spend a lot of time pestering yourself about the pastrami?

2. Explain in your own words how countenancing completely reasonable concerns can amount to unreasonable self-pestering.

3. If you were to create criteria by which to judge whether a given reasonable concern warrants your attention at a given moment and in given circumstances, how would you approach that task?

4. What does your characteristic negative self-talk sound like?

5. What would you like to try to do to eliminate much or all of your current self-pestering?

13

THE PAIN OF APPRAISING

We've looked at some of the disparate ways that a smart person, despite being smart, fails to notice that his brain has been lured away, that it's pestering him mercilessly, and that in other regards it seems not to see clearly what's going on. However, a smart person is also able to think clearly, at least some of the time. One of the results of thinking clearly, seeing clearly, and using his brain's available power is to see through the illogic and falsities around him—which produces a grave new set of problems.

First, it is alienating and upsetting to realize that the majority of people hold—and can be manipulated into holding—false and dangerous beliefs. If you know that the Earth revolves around the sun and if the authorities are putting people to death for holding that true belief, that is a calamity. If you can see through jingoist slogans and hack political arguments that are hijacking elections, that is likewise a calamity. Seeing clearly puts a given smart person at odds with his society; or, if he is another sort of smart person, it provides him with the means to cynically exploit the suckers around him.

That hundreds of millions of people believe that a man named Noah built an ark and put all of the world's species onto it two-by-two, that those species included dinosaurs—even though dinosaurs and man are separated by millions of years—that these people want this taught as science, that they want to get onto every school board and into every legislature to ensure that their view prevails, and that the mainstream media of a modern society continues to take this seriously, may only mildly annoy one smart person, perhaps one who grew up in religion and is tempted to give religion a pass. But it will seriously outrage—and almost derange—another smart person who is convinced that these views always come with an authoritarian edge and a coercive public agenda.

It will likewise strike a smart person as a ludicrous claim that the collectivist farms in her country are working beautifully when there is no food to be found on the shelves of any grocery store anywhere or to claim that a certain corporation is a mighty source for good and innovation when it is paying its employees peanuts and freely polluting. Misrepresentations of this sort affect our brain and our nervous system. They are an assault on our senses as well as our sense of right and wrong, and they bring pain and distress.

Of course, a given smart person may be participating in these falsehoods, invested in these falsehoods, and even the author of these falsehoods. We'll examine this matter in chapter 17 when we discuss the unfortunate truth that smart people do not form a community of virtue simply because they are smart. Smart people will distribute all along the spectrum of good and evil and can manifest as much blind self-interest as the next person. Here, in this chapter, I am picturing a smart person with progressive values who sees clearly at what great odds he finds himself with large segments of his society—whether the religious, the political, or the corporate—and who experiences pain as a result.

Second, his ability to see clearly will force him to see his *own* errors and shortfalls as well as the truth of his circumstances. He may simultaneously deny what he sees, as that defensiveness is entirely human also, but even as he works to deny what he is seeing, he is bound to be troubled by the fact that, for example, his beliefs do not hang together, that the house he is building is over budget, that the novel he is writing sags in the middle, that his son's explanations as to how he's been spending his time sound suspicious, and so on. If only in a corner of consciousness, these matters will plague him. He may try to get his blinders on as quickly as he can, but what he has seen has already registered.

Say, for example, that you decide to work for a company that makes lovely, inoffensive, harmless doodads that nobody really needs. You become their marketing manager and spend a million dollars a month promoting their doodad line. You can easily tally up the pluses of your choice: you have a lot of autonomy; you get to think about how to best market the doodad line, which makes use of your smarts; you rather like your coworkers; there is a nice lunch provided every day; and your boss isn't mean to you. All in all, the situation is just fine—except that you can't help noticing that it is completely meaningless to spend your time in support of these doodads.

You simultaneously understand why you are doing what you are doing as you see through what you are doing.

Then you go home and try to relax. Say you like action movies. Think of one of those action movies in which the hero, with whom we are manipulated into identifying, is getting away from the bad guys in a classic movie chase. Our hero is running for his life as cars crash all around him. Sometimes scores of people are injured or killed for no reason other than that our hero has the self-interested notion to save himself. In the context of movie reality, we root for him and ignore the carnage. In real life, if our son or daughter were killed in that melee, we would be much less willing to identify with that action hero and his needs. We might well want to say to him, "Give yourself up and spare those innocent people!"

In the context of movie reality, we are completely on his side—but in a corner of awareness, we see right through to the manipulation underneath. Not only may we suddenly stop enjoying the movie, but we may also get down on ourselves for our lapse in ethics and for wasting our time in the land of easy manipulation. *And* we may feel sad that we just lost one of our pleasures. Our ability to see through and to rightly appraise soured us on much of our day at work; now we are soured on our innocent evening pleasure.

Every time you step back and appraise, you are in danger of stepping into a self-pestering hole. The hole you've stepped into may amount to only a loss of what felt like an innocent pleasure, as in our action movie example. But every loss of joy makes us a bit sadder and a bit bleaker. You find a certain television personality charming, but you see right through to the fact that his show is a paean to gluttony. You enjoy taking a televised peek at beautiful houses, expensive yachts, and mega-vacations, but you see right through to the greed and the inequitable distribution of wealth that allow for such luxuries. There goes another simple pleasure and another idle entertainment!

One of the important consequences of this natural ability to appraise and to deconstruct is that you breed doubt in yourself. As a result of your ability to see through anything and everything, from your job choices to your entertainment choices to your views about the universe, you can end up mistrusting your own thoughts, your choices, your decisions, and even your values and principles. This vexing ability helps explain why smart people often seem indecisive and uncertain and, like Hamlet, have trouble knowing whether to be or not to be and whether to do or not to do. When you are good at deconstructing, you open the door to doubt.

The act of stepping back and appraising, which a good brain feels obliged to do as a moral imperative, reduces your ability to stand wholeheartedly behind anything. In war, if you step back and see your enemy as a person, that dramatically reduces your ability to shoot him without, however, contradicting what may be excellent reasons for shooting him. If he is trying to shoot you, it is not brilliant to construct a pacifist argument, to internally argue that privates are never responsible for their actions, or to feel some simple human kinship for him and his dilemma. That is a lot of pestering appraising to deal with when you have a split second to defend yourself.

You can see why appraising causes meaning drains. We were perhaps able to experience work as meaningful until we got to thinking about the senselessness of the doodads. We were perhaps able to experience our idle amusements as lovely vacations from meaning until we deconstructed them and experienced them not as vacations but as errors. We were perhaps able to experience our military service as meaningful until we thought too clearly about the other side's equally tenable positions. What we see when we step back and appraise is a purer vision of nature's ways, which can feel like a vision of the void. We become wiser, sadder, and more doubtful.

What can we do about what amounts to an inevitable, righteous, and sometimes useful ability to deconstruct that is simultaneously a self-pestering talent for pulling the rug out from under ourselves? What we can do is really learn the art of making value-based meaning. Unless we are very practiced at returning to our value-based meaning-making efforts at times of meaning crises, when even our values and our understanding of the world are called into question, we can doubt ourselves right into paralysis and despair. If, however, we are practiced at making value-based meaning, then we *know this is coming* and we know what to do: reconstruct the meaning that we just deconstructed.

If you just saw clearly that the novel you are writing is not good, you remind yourself that in your estimation, writing is one of your prime meaning opportunities and that you are obliged to make this novel better or else start a new novel. What you will not do is doubt writing, your writing intentions, or the universe. If you see through the action movie you are watching, you decide to close your eyes and enjoy it anyway, or you decide to move on with your day without recriminations or large doubts about meaning. What you do not do is turn your sensible desire to relax and your unfortunate vulnerability to manipulation into an indictment of you, your path, or the universe.

If you see through to the pointlessness of the doodads you sell, you smile that ironic smile that the situation warrants and decide to look for a new career, or else you enjoy the lovely lunch that's been provided while considering what meaning opportunities might supplement your not-too-meaningful day job. What you do not do is call life ridiculous and hate yourself, your bosses, and your choice or take your despair out on your children when you get home.

You look around you and you decide where and how to reinvest meaning or where and how to create new meaning. Side-by-side with your ability to appraise and deconstruct must sit an equally vibrant ability to reconstruct and repair meaning. Doubts come with the territory of being a smart human being and shouldn't surprise us, terrify us, or derail us. We simply make our next best guess—about, for example, whether we can spend another year selling doodads or not. And if we think yes, then we organize our attitude, our available personality, our idea of meaning, our additional meaning opportunities, and whatever else we need to organize into a team effort to make meaning in a world that includes doodads.

You may feel certain about your meaning choices and fiercely invested in your meaning choices. Or, just as likely, because you can appraise, deconstruct, and doubt, you may feel uncertain about your meaning choices and not particularly invested in your meaning choices. In that case, you must be doubly alert to the fact that you are responsible for the meaning in your life, that your doubts amount to meaning leaks, drains, and even crises, and that you must use your smarts to shore up meaning using the many principles and practices of natural psychology that are available to you.

For example, a useful practice in natural psychology is the morning meaning check-in. The idea is to spend a little time, as little as a few seconds, identifying for yourself what meaning investments you want to make on that day, what meaning opportunities you want to seize, and which parts of the day you want to designate as meaning neutral periods—that is, as periods that do not need to produce the psychological experience of meaning.

As part of your morning meaning check-in on a given day, you could, for example, make a decision about whether or not this is a day to countenance any deep appraising about your doodad job. If you decide that it isn't, you relax, accept your decision, look forward to some pleasant interactions with your coworkers and a good lunch, and commit to not pestering yourself about whether doodads hold meaning for you. If you decide that it is—if you decide that you really must tackle the meaninglessness of your doodad job—you articulate to yourself as clearly as you can what you intend to do: research a new job or a new career, talk to your boss about whether something of value can be added to the doodad, and so on.

On any given day, you have three choices with respect to your doodad job: you can be easy with it; you can name the concrete steps you intend to take to shore up meaning or make new meaning; or you can feel uncertain about it and start the day gloomy, unmotivated, and a little existentially nauseous. The last of these three is obviously the worst choice. It is much better to opt to reinvest in your current choice or to opt to make a new choice than to live upset and doubting.

In the first case, you shut off your appraising for the day (with that off switch that we wish we had but that we are endeavoring to cultivate through awareness training) and enjoy the day. If you opt for choice number one, you actually *stop pestering yourself* about your current choice: you use your awareness training and your cognitive skills to stop your brain from continuing its assault and from saddening you on what is otherwise a perfectly fine day. Nor do you want to let some small event serve as a trigger for renewed appraising and doubting. If, for example, you prefer French fries to coleslaw but lunch comes with coleslaw, that isn't reason enough to open up the debate about whether your job is meaningful enough. You've already decided that, for today, you will not engage in all that appraising, deconstructing, and doubting; therefore, you must not let coleslaw undo your hard-won decision.

In the second case, you decide to enjoy your day *and* to make some new meaning efforts, maybe by spending your lunch hour considering your next options (while enjoying that lovely lunch your work has provided).

A smart person, even if she can't help but see through, appraise, and deconstruct—even if her clear thinking puts her at odds with large segments of her society, and even if she has her doubts—can still energetically proceed in life.

She can leave Hamlet to pace alone on the ramparts of Elsinore. Her ability to appraise both serves her and pesters her, and that is the hand she has been dealt. She can see clearly; she can see too clearly; she can see too clearly too often. But she can also maintain a proud, unwavering commitment to making value-based meaning even as her values shift in the earthquakes of living.

CHAPTER QUESTIONS

1.   Is it your experience to see through life a lot?

2.   What are the positive and negative consequences of regular (or even constant) appraising and deconstructing?

3.   Can you dream up a way to reduce the negative consequences while retaining the positive ones?

4.   Does your penchant for appraising produce a great deal of doubt and, if it does, what can you do to doubt less or to better deal with the doubt generated?

5.   Does your seeing through, appraising, and deconstructing put you at odds with large segments of your society and, if it does, how do you want to deal with the resultant alienation, real-world difficulties, and perhaps outrage?

14

THE GOD-BUG SYNDROME

We have arrived at an interesting moment in the evolution of our species when a smart person in a first-world culture is pestered by two contradictory feelings: first that he is as special a creature as nature has yet produced and second that he's not very special at all, just excited matter here for a while and off again into universal dark matter.

This first feeling inflates him and makes him want to puff out his chest and preen a bit. This second feeling makes him want to crawl in a hole, act carelessly, or sit inert on the sofa. How unfortunate for a creature to be buffeted in such contradictory ways!

These twin feelings lead a person to the following pair of conclusions: that while he is perhaps quite smart, he is nevertheless rather like a cockroach, trapped with a brain that really isn't big enough for his purposes, perhaps trapped in a corner of an academic discipline, a research field, a literary genre, or in some other small place, trapped by his creatureliness, and trapped by life's very smallness.

I would like to dub this the god-bug syndrome: the prevalent and perhaps epidemic feeling of greatness walking hand-in-hand with smallness that plagues so many people today.

This is not, to use old-fashioned language, some sort of neurosis or neurotic belief. This is the quite sensible apprehension that there are two ways to look at life, as poignantly special and as pitiably worthless; that both views, while they clash, are entirely real and appropriate; and that a person can cycle between these two views almost minute by minute, feeling equal to life and up to life's challenges one second and pathetically inept and unequal to even thinking about making dinner the next.

This mix of reasonable self-pride and reasonable self-pity, in which what may be a completely healthy narcissistic attachment to one's own specialness collides with existential reality, produces people who look confident one moment and ineffectual the next, motivated one moment and apathetic the next, sober and hard-working one moment and self-indulgent and addicted the next. How can a person brim over with life energy and big plans one moment and feel suicidal the next? She can cycle exactly that way because of the god-bug syndrome.

It is startling that the same person can feel so grand and also so very small. Yet we see that picture all the time, as evidenced by the chronic sadness, mood swings, cycles of effort and lethargy, and secret self-soothing vices that so many smart people manifest. This college professor is famous for his theories and his addictions; this painter is exhibited everywhere and is a chronic hoarder at home; this physicist is brilliant by day and an insomniac night crawler; this lawyer can't be out-argued but has ballooned to three hundred pounds. This is the god-bug syndrome in action.

Traditional psychologies have considered this tension a disorder and have coined phrases like *delusions of grandeur* and *inferiority complex* to try to capture something of this so-called pathological dynamic. But at heart what we are talking about is not pathology but an intense conflictual knowing, a knowing that we are worthy smacking up against a knowing that we are just passing through: a knowing, that is, that we matter *and* that we do not matter. This is a true and not a pathological understanding. Every smart person possesses this understanding and can't help but feel distressed by this understanding.

In the past, this syndrome has indeed been pathologized. In the language of Adler, a disciple of Freud's, what we are looking at is a superiority complex driven by a hidden inferiority complex—or an inferiority complex driven by a hidden superiority complex. Adler put it this way: "We should not be astonished if in the cases where we see an inferiority complex we find a superiority complex more or less hidden. On the other hand, if we inquire into a superiority complex and study its continuity, we can always find a more or less hidden inferiority complex." Adler's god-bug is made up of two complexes. In natural psychology, we see this phenomenon as unfortunate and, in the existential sense, absurd—but we do not see it as a mental illness.

In natural psychology, we *expect* to see this. The self-inflation that Adler dubs a superiority complex and that the psychoanalytic thinker Karen Horney calls the idealization of the self, and the self-deflation that Adler names an inferiority complex and that Horney identifies as the despised self—each in their estimation located in a walled-off unconscious place that puts the person out of touch with his self-inflations and his self-deflations—in natural psychology we see instead as the quite reasonable outgrowth of the experience of singularity and uniqueness, on the one hand, and contingency and shortfalls, on the other.

We *are* god-bugs. That is the nature of this current experimental model of our species.

Natural psychology also proposes a way out of this dilemma—or, if not a way out of it, a way to deal with it as effectively as it can be dealt with. If you construct an idea of meaning that takes these very matters into account, so that both your next accomplishment and your next disappointment are accounted for in your personal picture of value-based meaning-making, you can get off your high horse and you can also get up from the dirt. By taking charge of your construction of meaning, you can maintain a steady identity, one characterized by a new modesty *and* a new strength.

Your brain can conceptualize ideas as abstract as the relationship between energy and matter; it can produce strings of words and strings of musical notes that evoke tremendous feeling; it can place itself in the vast universe and see itself living and dying. It can imagine, calculate, remember, and more. It has to feel special. At the same time, it knows perfectly well all about its limitations and its fleeting nature. This god-bug syndrome is completely natural and exactly what you would expect a creature like us to experience. Now we must deal with it.

Why Smart People Hurt

Here are two reports that illustrate this distressing natural phenomenon. Sandra explained:

> My parents always told me that I was very bright—that everyone in our family was very bright but that I shined the brightest. Maybe this ought to have pleased me, but I didn't really feel all that bright, not compared to the kids at school who were super-quick at math or super-quick at memorizing and especially not compared to the geniuses I would read about both in school and in my spare time. I got a little obsessed with reading about all those geniuses because I had this powerful doubt that I was anything like them, and I guess I wanted to confirm that to myself.

> So I thought to myself, *Where can you be smart but you don't have to be really super-smart?* I decided that I would become a concert pianist. That sounded so cultured and, even if it wasn't the doctor or lawyer my parents wanted me to become, it was at least in a category of jobs where I'd associate with doctors and lawyers. I knew even then as a little girl that I was making a very odd decision, one that had to do with feeling somewhat special but also not feeling special enough to try something amazing. So I ended up choosing something that was perhaps the very hardest thing I could

have chosen, because I didn't love practicing and I had performance anxiety.

I played pretty well, people praised me, I ended up going to a good music school, and part of me started to feel a bit grand—I even remember how I would put down other instruments and music that wasn't classical and all sorts of things—and I think that most people probably found me a little bit arrogant. At the same time, I didn't really feel like anything special at all. I felt more like an awkward, unfocused, lonely person on some pretty meaningless path.

Finally—and fortunately—I began to see that I would never become a great solo concert performer, and I had a breakdown of sorts. But I would have to say that I almost needed that breakdown, that I had been living an odd lie, and that all of those questions about whether I was great or nothing really had to get answered in some sensible way if I was to continue to have some sort of life. I had a bad year and even had to go back home to live, where of course I kept hearing about how it wasn't at all too late for me to become a lawyer and how easy it would be for me, since I was so smart.

During the course of that hard time I began to see what had been going on. I wasn't

Why Smart People Hurt

either a diva or a failure. I was simply a person, one who didn't know herself very well and who needed to deeply change her relationship to life. I started thinking not just about the things I could do but also about the ways I could be. I concerned myself not so much with my next job but with the idea of me being the best me I could be. At the same time, I made the adamant decision that I wouldn't get too enthusiastic *or* too dismissive about my prospective choices. I wanted to just think calmly about how my future might look. This took many months of thinking—fortunately, I had my parents' home and resources to support me during this period of reflection.

What I realized was that I wanted love and a life and to be of a little help in the world. That sounds so simple, but its modesty was very new to me. I found myself smiling. I didn't need to be super-great, and I also didn't need to be nothing. I decided to start a small business playing the piano (actually a keyboard that I could take with me places) and talking about women composers to any group that wanted to hear me. I'd go to elementary schools, retirement homes, even big conferences. And what happened was, I actually fell in love with the music.

There was little money to be made from this beautiful work, and I really couldn't have continued it without the independent income I have from a trust fund set up by my parents. I understand exactly how privileged that makes me, but that truth doesn't send me either to the diva place in me or to the failure place in me. My path makes sense to me—it is a useful, authentic, and good-feeling way to live a life. I have additional things that I want to try to be the human being that I want to be, but I'm also convinced that I've made a decent start.

Jared, a computer engineer, explained:

I grew up knowing that I could really do math. I had that kind of mind. That was clear to me from a very early age. I could do any sort of computational problem in my mind faster and better than anyone else. I was proud of that ability and pretty puffed up about it. At the same time, I had zero common sense or attunement to what was going on around me. My parents could keep any secret from me they wanted—I was just completely unaware. You could easily have sold me the Brooklyn Bridge. And I knew that about myself exactly as well as I knew that I could compute. So both powerful feelings built up in me, that I was singular and great and that I was also wretched, embarrassingly naïve, and somehow unlovable because of my awkwardness and unmanliness.

I remember making lists of how I could be more like a man or acquire more common sense or be more aware of my surroundings. It was pathetic. I was pathetic. My clothes were ridiculous. The way I wore my hair was ridiculous. But I was a whiz in school, won everything that could be won, and was on my way to some high-paying computer job or, even loftier, some start-up idea that might make me billions. The kids around me sort of intuited that about me, that I was a pathetic loser who might also become a billionaire—and their employer. It was weird. I was both a pariah and put on a pedestal.

I had a miserable college time, but life started to get better when I got out into the real world—where my thinking skills were actually valued. But although things got better because I was valued and because I could spread my wings, I was still pretty miserable with respect to anything that wasn't related to computers or start-ups. I drank too much, even though I had no desire to drink, and I ate too much—that was my real place of self-soothing. I had no girlfriends, no real friends, and no connection to anything going on in the world.

Worst of all, I started collecting comic books. That felt pathetic and ridiculous, and I knew that I was becoming a kind of crazy hoarder. Then one day I had a realization. I realized that I had taken the path of least resistance by focusing on my mind and not my heart. A light went on. I sold all my comic books— no single act in my life has ever felt better. I joined a dating service and, although I felt like an idiot every time I went out, I did go out. Slowly, over time, I felt myself becoming a person. Well, to tell the honest truth, it was even more than that—I began to feel like a man. Making money was never the issue; living was. Now I am on the tougher path of actually living.

There are countless opportunities for a smart person to puff up a bit and begin to incline in the direction of arrogance, grandiosity, and unhealthy narcissism. At the same time, there are an equal or greater number of opportunities for a smart person to feel minimized, inferior, helpless, and completely unimportant. That ironic smirk or sarcastic smile that a smart person sometimes can't help but turn toward the world can turn in an instant into a grimace of pain as she plummets from a grand sense of self to a much lowlier feeling.

What might help alleviate this pain would be smart people supporting one another. But smart people do not make a village. The 1.5 billion people who constitute the top smartest 15 percent of the world's population do not amount to an affinity group. They are diverse and, while perhaps quick at addition or imaginative or good at abstraction, they are not brothers and sisters, not by a long shot.

One smart person will devote himself to radical selfishness, and another smart person will feel compassion for her fellow human beings. One smart person will find himself tied in knots by anxiety, and another smart person will feel little anxiety and wonder if the anxiety her friends complain about is even real. One smart person will experience no particular meaning problems and fall right into a life that brings him the psychological experience of meaning with such regularity that he has no idea why there's so much fuss about meaning—while another smart person will experience chronic, severe problems with meaning. Smart people are all over the map.

They find themselves on the right and on the left and everywhere in between, in every profession and manifesting every personality trait. As Mensa, the organization for bright people, puts it: "There is simply no one prevailing characteristic of Mensa members other than high IQ. . . . As far as occupations, the range is staggering. Mensa has professors and truck drivers, scientists and firefighters, computer programmers and farmers, artists, military people, musicians, laborers, police officers, glassblowers—the diverse list goes on and on." It goes on to include every sort of human being imaginable.

Nothing in particular ties this 1.5 billion–person conglomerate together except a certain endowment. Just as tall people do not form an affinity group just by virtue of being tall, smart people do not form an affinity group just by virtue of being smart. Like tall people, who may share certain challenges—they need to watch out for the blades of fans and for low doorjambs and have to tolerate the question, "Do you play basketball?"—smart people also share certain challenges. That, after all, is the premise of this book. But that they share certain challenges doesn't make them a village.

This fact, that the next smart person you meet is not only not automatically a friend or a compatriot but may hold beliefs diametrically opposed to yours and may even prove to be your enemy, produces additional pain. Many smart people pine for community, even as they recognize that they themselves do not necessarily make good villagers and even as they realize with some chagrin that while they support humane institutions, they do not particularly enjoy people. They suppose that other smart people might constitute that community they seek—and that they don't is at once another inflation and another deflation. Without that village, you are once again singular and small.

What is the short answer as to what to do? Countenance neither feeling and neither state. Just as you want meaning to trump mood as you spend more time making meaning than monitoring your moods, you want meaning to trump identity. You want to spend more time making meaning than locating yourself on some scale of importance. You are not at one end or the other end of that scale: you are simply (and quite importantly enough) a human being. That is the short answer—we will look at the longer answer shortly.

Why Smart People Hurt

CHAPTER QUESTIONS

1. Have you experienced this god-bug dynamic?

2. What are your thoughts about what you might try to heal it or change it?

3. Do you incline more toward the god side or the bug side of this dynamic?

4. If you do incline more toward one side or the other, what are your thoughts on the reasons for this inclination?

5. If you would prefer not to be a god-bug, what sort of human being would you prefer to be?

15

COMING TO GRIPS WITH MEANING

If you are smart, you are likely to have more problems with meaning than the next person because of your ability to form abstract ideas, appreciate the existential nature of reality, appraise the workings of the universe, and so on. If, however, you come to understand the exact nature of meaning, meaning can become that much less of a problem for you.

You can finally stop pining for meaning to be something different from what it actually is, settle in to making value-based meaning on a daily basis, and let go of the need to seek meaning or impatiently wait for meaning to arrive. As a result, you become the arbiter of meaning in your life and, by so doing, reduce your distress and begin to solve many of the problems we've discussed so far.

Natural psychology holds the following views on meaning. Meaning is first of all and primarily a mere psychological experience. When our running subjective experience has a certain resonant quality to it—maybe it's a feeling of rightness, maybe it's an oceanic quality, maybe it's some integrative quality, maybe it's an experience of significance, maybe it's an experience of joy or pleasure—we have the sensation that life possesses meaning. This is the psychological experience of meaning. At such times, life feels like it matters, makes sense, is all right, and so on.

Because human beings aren't trained to notice these as experiences of meaning and because we don't possess a robust vocabulary of meaning, we often don't notice that we've just had the psychological experience of meaning. We might spend an afternoon walking the back streets of a French town wearing a smile because something has been stirred in us by the experience and nevertheless not *credit* that afternoon as a psychological experience of meaning. We *had* the experience, but we didn't quite know to label it as such or to credit it as such. For this reason, the majority of our psychological experiences of meaning pass by unnoticed and in a certain sense discredited.

This is a vital point to remember because when you engage in the process of evaluating life as meaningful enough or not meaningful enough, an idea that we'll get to in a moment, it is easy to evaluate life as a cheat and not meaningful enough because you haven't been noticing or crediting all those passing psychological experiences of meaning. Life is likely more meaningful than you thought it was—but you may not have noticed.

These psychological experiences of meaning can arise unbidden, or they may arise because we actively invited them. You might have business in that French town and have that psychological experience of meaning come to you unbidden, by virtue of you being there accidentally. Or you might enjoy that afternoon of meaning *because* you actively made the decision to travel there and because you had the suspicion, which proved accurate, that your time there would provoke the experience of meaning. That is, without any guarantees in place and strictly on a hunch, you booked that trip to France as a meaning-making effort and you were rewarded with the experience of meaning. In the first case, you had meaning arise unbidden; in the second case, you arrived there on purpose and, by having taken the necessary action to turn your intention into reality, you made meaning.

Next, we come to the idea of meaning as *evaluation*. Why might we not credit a given psychological experience as meaningful, even if it was? We might not credit the experience as meaningful because we may have already evaluated *life itself* as meaningless, as a cheat, a fraud, and so on. Measuring all of our experiences against that background negative evaluation, we may have gotten in the unfortunate habit of dismissing all our experiences as meaningless. To put it aphoristically, no experience can feel meaningful to a nihilist—that is, to someone who has already decided that life is meaningless.

Consider as an analogy the following. If, because you've experienced too much pain or been disappointed too many times, you decide that nothing in life can ever feel genuinely enjoyable, then you will instantly sour experiences that might have had the chance of being experienced as joyful. You will continually pour rain on your own parade. How we evaluate life matters because we experience life against the backdrop of our evaluation of life. If that evaluation is negative, nothing has much of a chance of feeling positive. Indeed, a lot of what gets labeled as the *mental disorder of depression* is in fact a persistent negative evaluation of life.

Why might you evaluate life that harshly? Maybe because you went unloved as a child, maybe because you have to spend a stupendous amount of your time just earning a living, maybe because you never met your soul mate, maybe because you see immorality rewarded and good deeds punished, maybe because you had dreams that never materialized and goals that you never met, maybe because you had just expected *more* out of life—more from it, more from others, more from yourself. Add on all the smart challenges we've discussed so far and I think you can see how easy and natural it is to evaluate life as a cheat—maybe easier and more natural than evaluating it as something worth the candle.

A great many people have evaluated life this way, without, however, realizing that they have made that decision and without realizing how many unfortunate consequences flow from that decision. One of the ways that an adherent of natural psychology makes meaning is by refusing to evaluate life negatively even though she has ample reasons to do so. Even though you have ample reasons to feel that life is a cheat, you must, for the sake of experiencing meaning, evaluate life as worth living. You must decide that life matters, that your efforts matter, and that you matter. Can you manage to evaluate life in a positive way even though you've been badly disappointed in the past and even though you find life taxing and unrewarding? That is a conversation that you must have with yourself. You must air this question and with

Why Smart People Hurt

luck come down on the side of deciding that life matters *despite everything.*

The psychological experience of meaning will not want to arise in you if you've made certain negative calculations about life or if you've decided that unless life looks like x—say, fair—or provides you with y—say, success—you will consider it a cheat. How charming will a sweet little cottage feel if you have in mind that you were supposed to live in a castle? How much meaning can you extract from a solid paragraph of writing if you had in mind that you were supposed to write great novels? Your own experiences of meaning may not amount to enough or serve you well enough if you evaluate life as requiring more than it has so far offered you or more than it *can* offer.

This is not the same as saying that an adherent of natural psychology learns to settle. Rather, he tries to think this all through, recognizing that he is dealing with his own personality, his own desires, his own habits of mind, and his own fears as he tries to thoughtfully make these calculations and evaluations. Because he knows that how he evaluates life colors how he perceives his experiences, that his evaluation provides him or fails to provide him with moment-by-moment motivation, and that his evaluation determines whether or not he will bother to live according to his principles, he attempts the odd work of thoughtfully deciding if he can possibly evaluate life more positively. Maybe, just maybe, he can find the way to do that—maybe, that is, he can come down on the side of affirming that life matters.

Because we human beings wall off knowledge that upsets us, we may well not know that we have evaluated life as pointless, a cheat, and a fraud. We may diligently farm our small farm or show up at the office every day and refuse to notice that we find our life absurd. It might be expected that we would get some clues from our behaviors—that we drink a lot, that we take antidepressants, that we fantasize about taking our revenge—but rather than drawing any logical conclusions from our behaviors, we continue going through the motions. A great many people, and especially our smartest, have come to negative conclusions and evaluations about life but, supposing that it can do them no good to notice or because they are too embarrassed to notice, deny that they have given life a thumbs-down.

An adherent of natural psychology believes that it does a person good to notice—great good—even if that noticing brings pain. She knows that if she has evaluated life as a cheat, as a fraud, as pointless and ridiculous, then she is bound to dismiss out-of-hand her psychological experiences of meaning as even less than mere experiences—she will dismiss them as the merest of experiences. She will even use them as evidence that life is a cheat, providing, as they do, proof that nothing but occasional experiences of a certain sort exist in what is otherwise a vast sea of meaninglessness.

If, on the other hand, you paint a different sort of picture for yourself, one in which you conceptualize life not as a cheat and a fraud but as a project, an obligation, an opportunity to make yourself proud, and even as an adventure, you will discover that you experience meaning more often and that those experiences of meaning begin to count. Furthermore, holding to this new, positive view, you realize that meaning can even begin to recede as an issue—that in order to make yourself proud, you are obliged to focus on manifesting your values and your principles and, when you do that, the problem of meaning begins to vanish.

Next is the matter of meaning as an idea. Human beings, but smart people especially, are able to think and to form abstract ideas. They not only can feel joy, but they can also conceptualize the *idea* of joy. Likewise, they not only can experience meaning, but they can also conceptualize the *idea* of meaning.

How you conceptualize meaning matters. If you hold that it is outside of yourself and must be tracked down, you have one idea of meaning. If, however, you conceive of it as I've been describing it—that it is a subjective experience, that it sometimes comes unbidden and that it can also be coaxed into existence, that when it is absent we must try to create it rather than search for it, and so on—then you are holding a very different idea of meaning. It should go without saying that what sort of idea you hold about meaning matters a great deal—in fact, it completely dictates how you will live your life. How you construe meaning dictates how you will live your life.

The way you construe meaning affects everything, from how much pleasure you get from ordinary things to how sincere an effort you make in manifesting your values and your principles. I think that the idea of meaning that I'm promoting, by being true-to-life and by returning meaning to your hands, will help you live more intentionally, more richly, and more happily. Be that as it may, *you* get to form *your* idea of meaning—and whatever you decide about meaning dictates how you will live.

Remember that life is not set up to meet our meaning needs. It only sporadically provides us with the experience of meaning. Yes, we can endeavor to make our meaning—and we should make that effort. But those efforts come with no guarantees, and it may happen that we may not be able to produce the experience of meaning often enough. Consider the following situation: You find yourself in a job that bores you, and sixty hours of your week are taken up with experiences that do not provide the experience of meaning. You also find yourself in a relationship that isn't working, and those hours with your mate also fail to provide the experience of meaning. A person in this situation is going to experience meaning as a tremendous challenge, since virtually all of her hours are taken up with experiences that do not provide much or any meaning.

Meaning is a challenge in a second sense as well. As soon as you so-to-speak burden an experience with the need that it feel meaningful, you likely reduce its ability to provide that psychological experience. Let's say that you begin writing a novel because it wells up in you to write that novel. You don't think about whether or not writing your novel is going to prove meaningful—you just start writing. *That* experience is entirely likely to provide you with the psychological experience of meaning. Say, however, that you are hungry for meaning and make the conscious decision that writing a novel will be one of your meaning-making activities and that you expect that working on it will provide you with the psychological experience of meaning. In this case, and ironically enough, you may be less likely to experience meaning. A self-conscious demand on an activity that it *feel meaningful* is likely to reduce its chances of actually feeling meaningful.

You want to make meaning, but you also do not want to burden your efforts with the demand that they *feel* meaningful. This is not a paradox but rather a matter of outlook. You can *hope* that something will provide you with the experience of joy without attaching to it the *need* that it provide you with that experience. You can hope that the vacation you take will prove enjoyable, maybe by virtue of all of the sunbathing you intend to do, without *needing* the vacation to prove enjoyable. Then if it happens to rain every day while you are there, you may still be able to enjoy the vacation because you weren't attached to all that sunbathing. Similarly, you can *hope* that a given meaning opportunity will produce the experience of meaning without attaching to *needing* it to produce that experience.

You can't force life to meaning, and you don't want to try to force life to meaning. Rather, you want to make conscious decisions about what efforts you think amount to value-based meaning-making efforts, and then you want to *relax*. This deep relaxation is a philosophical stance that translates as the following: "I choose to do this next thing because I see it as a thing of value; and who knows what will happen." The meaning-making is in the choosing, the valuing, and the doing—and whatever happens, happens. By remembering that this is what making meaning involves, you will experience a sense of pride at having chosen, valued, and done something even if you don't happen to experience meaning from the activity itself.

Meaning is a tremendous challenge in precisely this sense—that while we use phrases like *making meaning* and *creating meaning*, what we are really advocating for is a certain sort of effort because we can't guarantee a certain sort of result. An adherent of natural psychology, calculating what she values and what matters to her, points herself in the direction of meaning, makes the requisite effort, and then relaxes. Natural psychology starts with the premise that human beings are built to experience virtually anything as meaningful but that we respect ourselves *more* when the meaning we experience arises because we have followed our values and principles rather than because meaning arose unbidden in us. That is, the principled meaning that we mindfully make is our most valuable meaning. There is a great deal in this view of meaning for a smart person to apply to help meet the challenges we've discussed so far.

Why Smart People Hurt

CHAPTER QUESTIONS

1. Natural psychology views meaning as primarily a subjective psychological experience. If you agree with this view, what do you see as its implications for living?

2. If you disagree with this view, what is your view?

3. What implications for living flow from your view?

4. If you agree that it makes sense to create a robust idea of meaning, what would yours be?

5. If you sense that you are currently evaluating life negatively, to what extent would you like to reevaluate life as mattering more?

16

MAKING DAILY MEANING

I f you agree with natural psychology's view that meaning is primarily a subjective psychological experience
(powerfully affected by a person's idea of meaning and
her evaluation of life as meaningful or not), if you further agree that what follows from this observation is
the realization that you can make meaning (or at least
significantly influence its arrival), and if you also agree
that nothing is really more important than making and
maintaining that meaning, then it follows that you will
want to make meaning on a daily basis. What follows are
fifteen tips for doing exactly that.

Orient Yourself

First thing each day, orient yourself in the direction of
meaning. Rather than starting your day by worrying
about your daily tasks and everything looming ahead of
you, rather than orienting yourself toward your day job
and your everyday pursuits, spend a minute or two quietly
and calmly asking yourself, "Where do I intend to make
meaning today?"

You look at your day and you thoughtfully make decisions about where you want to invest meaning. This process sounds like: "I'm investing an hour first thing on building my home business, then I'm adopting a calm attitude as I commute to work, then at work I'm staying in meaning neutral for most of the day except for my morning meeting with Bill, where I want to invest myself and aim for a certain outcome. Then more calmness as I commute home, and then a nice vacation from meaning and a little enjoyment as I cook and listen to music, and then an hour investment in my business and a ten-minute investment in a quick call to my sister. Then a final meaning investment in peaceful sleep as I go to bed calmly and sleep like a baby!" As long as it took you to read all that, it would take you hardly a second or two to *think* it—after which, you would be nicely oriented toward the meanings of your day.

Maintain One Main Morning Practice

Maintain one ongoing meaning investment of the doing sort or of the being sort, which you attend to first thing each morning, before your so-to-speak real day begins. In this way, you make meaning first thing each day, and that effort builds up meaning capital over time, significantly inoculating you against meaning crises.

Although the distinction between being and doing is artificial, the following will give you a sense of what I mean. Being practices might include sitting meditation, walking meditation, tai chi, or yoga, even though all of them also have a doing component. Doing practices might include writing your novel, building your home business, working your recovery program, working your anxiety management program, and so on, even though each of them also has a being component.

You can choose any prospective meaning opportunity and practice it first thing each morning. Over time, this becomes the place where you make an ongoing meaning investment in a regular, routine, daily way.

Take Direct Aim at Your Greatest Meaning Challenge

You may hold writing your novel, building your home business, or nurturing your relationships as your greatest meaning opportunity but simultaneously hold staying sober, dealing with your meaningless job, or handling some aspect of your formed personality as your greatest meaning challenge. Take daily aim at these meaning challenges.

If, for example, your greatest meaning challenge is that you manage to form rich intentions but then fail to align your thoughts and behaviors with those intentions, then you would mindfully take aim at aligning your thoughts and behaviors with your intentions. You would announce to yourself every day how you were going to do exactly that. This might sound like: "I want to create that nonprofit I've been dreaming about for fifteen years, and so today I am going to create a couple of thoughts that support my intention and think them every hour on the hour. I'm also going to take the first baby steps in the direction of starting my nonprofit by buying some nonprofit guides and by chatting with Jill about how she started her nonprofit."

In addition to seizing meaning opportunities on a daily basis, you also take direct aim at your greatest meaning challenges on a daily basis. You name your greatest meaning challenge, rather than ignoring it and refusing to think about it, and then you announce what you are going to do to meet that challenge *today*.

Make Meaning in Context

Each day is its own context, each hour is its own context, and each minute is its own context. That's why now is at once so rich and so difficult! It is a particular now that must be lived on its own terms and as its own situation.

It may not prove meaningful for you to sit for two hours on a bench in front of your supermarket. But it may prove wonderfully meaningful for you to sit for two hours on a bench in front of a small grocery store while you're traveling the back roads of Italy. Those are quite different contexts. The same activity might provoke the psychological experience of meaning in one context and not in another. Working on your novel might be the thing to do, come hell or high water—but if your child falls down and skins her knee, then attending to her and not working on your novel is clearly the thing to do.

Three p.m. today when your boss says something rude to you in a slightly more injurious way than usual, speaking up may be the thing to do—or keeping silent may be the thing to do. That will be its own situation with its own particularities and you will get to make meaning right then and there, on the spot, in *that* situation. Life is a series of unique situations, and we make meaning not by adhering to abstract principles about how we should live but according to the reality of each moment.

Look Ahead

Take notice throughout your day of the time looming up ahead of you and announce to yourself how you want to be with it—how you want to be with that meeting that's coming up in five minutes, how you want to be with your lunch hour, how you want to be as you settle in to return a difficult email. You surveyed the day first thing that morning and made certain decisions, which was a great practice; now the living day is transpiring in real time, and you need to make new decisions as new situations present themselves.

Like many of the other practices I've been describing, this activity of noticing and announcing takes only a second. It isn't a burdensome practice that takes a lot of time but rather is a practiced instantaneous check-in with yourself in which, for example, you remind yourself that you want to be calm or assertive or a little extra attentive or meaning neutral. In a microsecond, you make meaning by adding a bit of mindful attention to the current situation or an upcoming situation.

Define Free Time

Remember that free time is not necessarily easy time. Those two hours in the evening when you have "nothing to do" and can do "whatever you want" need to be treated as mindfully, carefully, and seriously as any other two hours of your life.

You can spend them calmly in meaning neutral, if you like, but on some evenings, that will not be the way you actually want to spend those two hours. Trying to spend them that way will leave you bored and upset and in a mini-meaning crisis. Free time is time that must be treated with as much consideration as all other time.

Allow Easiness

All of this consideration, thoughtfulness, and effort in no way preclude the possibility of spontaneity, relaxation, just being, and other easier ways of being. In fact, life may get easier if you are living as an adherent of natural psychology because, on the one hand, you have a good idea of how you want to represent yourself and make yourself proud, and on the other hand, you know that you have permission not to struggle all the time with meaning. In this way, you get the best of both possible worlds: a clear picture of what you're intending and a clear picture that you need not struggle to make every moment feel meaningful.

On a given day, this can play itself out as an hour of intentional meaning-making, followed by a complete opening to whatever wants to happen, followed by some more hours of intentional meaning-making, followed by great and sublime ease. By not feeling like you're on some endless quest, as a seeker of meaning does, you can take it easy any time you like. Indeed, you may want to devote a portion of every day to this deep ease.

Invest in Being

You do not need to invest meaning only in activities like building your business, writing your novel, being of service, or relating. You can also invest meaning in a particular way of being. That is, you can choose a way of being—say, being calm, being open, being compassionate, and so on—and invest meaning in being that way.

On a given day, this might mean the following: You might decide that your only goal for the afternoon is to remain calm. You see an array of stressors on the horizon for the afternoon, and you decide that what will serve you the most is dealing with them calmly—that being calm is the work. Maybe this means doing something like practicing an anxiety management technique or aligning your thoughts with your intention. But as the afternoon unfolds, it is all about being and not doing—it is about actually being calm. Remember that mindfully adopting an *attitude* is as much a feature of making meaning as is mindfully choosing an activity.

Think Thoughts that Serve You

You have ongoing cognitive work to do to keep your thoughts aligned with your intentions. This work has a daily face to it as, today and every day, you make sure that you are thinking thoughts that serve you and disputing thoughts that do not serve you.

If, for example, you intend to make meaning by starting your home business and you hear yourself saying, "Wow, there's just too much to do," right then and there, stop and remind yourself to what extent that thought fails to serve you. Right then and there, substitute a thought that *does* serve you and that aligns with your meaning-making intentions, a thought like, for example, *Okay, what am I tackling first?*

This is daily work and in-the-moment work, as it is in the moment that the thoughts that don't serve us appear. Again, this tip takes many words to say, but in actuality it will take you hardly a second to notice a thought that isn't serving you, dispute it, and substitute one that does serve you—hardly a second, that is, if you get in the habit of doing it.

Behave in Ways that Serve You

You have ongoing behavioral work to do to keep your actions aligned with your intentions. This work also has a daily face to it as, today and every day, you behave in ways aligned with your intentions and as you refuse to behave in ways not aligned with your intentions.

Say you're building your home business and need a quote from someone regarding a web-building service. In your possession are three names to contact. The obvious behavior that aligns with your intention is to prepare your questions for these three people and then to contact them. As straightforward as that sounds, many if not most people will do other things so as to avoid the anxiety that naturally arises in such situations.

They'll tell themselves that they need five names rather than only three. They'll tell themselves that they need to become a kind of mini-expert on the subject and order three books before calling anyone. They'll tell themselves that although they've already figured out that they can't perform the service themselves, they will take a class to see if maybe they can learn to perform it. Instead of doing the thing that they know they ought to do, namely contacting those three people, they decide to do something else instead.

Every day, we must watch out that we aren't tricking ourselves into performing actions that aren't aligned with our intentions.

Make Daily Use of Your Available Personality

Remember that we have an original personality that we can never discern clearly, a formed personality that tends to restrict our freedom, and a certain amount of personality left, our available personality, with which we maintain self-awareness, calculate our meaning intentions, and manifest our freedom.

Every day, you call on your available personality to provide you with the means to realize your intentions. If you fall back on your formed personality and live life in a rote, mechanical way, you will repeat what failed to work in the past and you will stay as anxious, sad, and ineffective as you're accustomed to staying.

If you remind yourself each day that you want to lead with your strongest self, your smartest self, and your freest self, you give yourself the chance to realize the meaning intentions you form. Whether you call your available personality your best self, your highest self, or something else—or whether you give it no name at all—it alone provides you with the means to your ends. You can't be the value-based meaning-maker you would like to be unless you manifest your available personality in a daily way.

Check in on Meaning Opportunities

Once you've created a menu of meaning opportunities—that is, a menu of those things that matter to you or that match your idea of what constitutes value-based meaning-making—double-check that list, either daily or at least regularly. Try something on that list that you haven't tried recently or something high on that list that you keep avoiding. By checking your list, you remind yourself of all the meaning opportunities available to you—a reminder that amounts to its own sort of meaning boost. First, of course, you will need to create your list of meaning opportunities.

Human beings experience any and all of the following fifteen as meaning opportunities: love, good works, creativity, excellence, relationships, stewardship, experimentation, pleasure, self-actualization, service, career, contentment, ethical action, achievement, and appreciation. But of course your list must be your list. Parenting might be high on your list; parenting might appear nowhere on your list. Achieving might matter more to you than loving; loving might matter more to you than achieving. Check in with yourself regularly to see if you want to seize a meaning opportunity that you've been forgetting or avoiding.

Stop Up Meaning Leaks

Take quick action when a meaning leak occurs. Say that you run into your brother, who reminds you that you don't make much money at your career and will probably always be financially stressed. This may amount to an emotional blow, but it is also a meaning blow, and the meaning can leak out of your chosen profession if you take his words to heart.

On the one hand, you will need to deal with having just been emotionally battered. But you will also need to deal with the meaning part, maybe by mindfully reinvesting meaning in your profession right there on the spot. This might sound like, "Yes, poetry doesn't pay, but I'm a poet and that's how I make my meaning." Or, "Yes, corporate law would certainly pay more than the legal aid work I do, but I make my meaning by serving." As often as every day, a meaning drain or a meaning leak can occur. Therefore it is our daily work to deal with them instantly and on the spot.

Deal with Special Circumstances

Not only do you want to take quick action when a meaning leak or a meaning drain occurs, but you also want to remain alert to any special blows or circumstances that may affect your relationship to meaning.

Maybe, for example, you've been able to tolerate your day job because you like your boss. When a new, crueler boss takes over, that may amount to a special blow and may kill off the possibility of your job ever providing you with the psychological experience of meaning. These special circumstances must be dealt with as and when they occur.

Weeks and months may pass during which nothing dramatic occurs. But on a day when something dramatic *does* occur, it is your job to give your undivided attention to its reality and decide what you want to do to remedy or repair the situation. Maybe there's cognitive work to do, or maybe you'll need to take action. The idea of making meaning includes taking necessary action to deal with meaning crises and meaning challenges *as soon as* they occur.

Practice

Consider all of life as your practice and each day as a day to practice. Since your goal, if you agree that it is your goal, is to engage in value-based meaning-making, then the shorthand for your entire practice might be something like: doing the next right thing. Right in the phrase doing the next right thing doesn't precisely mean "ethical" or "moral" but something more complicated. It translates roughly as doing the next appropriate thing in the context of your life as your project.

This might sound like: "I see life as a complicated project in which sometimes I enjoy myself, sometimes I exhaust myself in the service of my work, sometimes I take vacations from meaning, sometimes I strive to satisfy my ambitions, sometimes I stop everything and seize an unexpected meaning opportunity, and so on. My daily practice is to mindfully manage this complicated thing that is the project of my life." Every single day is the next day in the project that is your life.

If there is one steady, regular, overarching thing that you can do to deal with the challenges of being smart, it is making meaning on a daily basis. You do this arduous, important work even as meaning shifts—which is our next subject.

CHAPTER QUESTIONS

1. What do you see as the relationship between making meaning on a daily basis and handling the challenges of being smart?

2. Can you identify one challenge from the many that we've discussed—the anxiety of thinking, the difficulties of finding smart enough work, the self-pestering nature of our inner talk, an inability to land on anything of genuine interest, and so on—that you think might be ameliorated by making meaning on a daily basis?

3. What do you think you might choose as your morning practice?

4. I've described starting the day with a morning meaning check-in. What are your thoughts about ending the day in the same way?

5. What do you suppose might stand in the way of you making meaning on a daily basis?

17

EMBRACING SHIFTING MEANINGS

There are many ways of dealing with the challenges that come with being smart, and each challenge requires a different sort of response. One overarching response, however, is taking better care of meaning and engaging in value-based meaning-making. In the previous chapter, I provided several tips for making daily meaning. In this chapter, I want to continue our chat and describe how you can deal with meaning shifting on you.

Natural psychology begins with a splash of cold water by identifying meaning as primarily a subjective psychological experience. But it follows that icy start with the assertion that meaning is a *regularly available* psychological experience, as available as any other. And it continues with the notion that you can form a potent idea about meaning—your own definition of meaning, as it were, one that helps you make powerful decisions about life, including the decision to live life with pride. Meaning arises because it is natural for it to arise, and we do not need to pine for some other supposedly better or bigger meaning connected to wishful thinking about a more purposeful universe.

An adherent of natural psychology thinks in the following way: *I sense that many things have the ability to provoke the psychological experience of meaning in me. One is pleasure. Another is achievement. Another is ego gratification. Another is just being. Another is acting in accordance with my values. And so on. As I think about this, I see that while I want and need the psychological experience of meaning, it also matters how I acquire it. I would prefer not to acquire it in ways that run counter to my values and that make me feel disappointed in myself. I am in the position of making the bold decision to create value-based goals and to chase value-based dreams—while at the same time allowing myself pleasure, ego gratification, and anything and everything else that produces the psychological experience of meaning.*

This is a considerably more complicated self-chat than concluding, "I want a dance career," "I believe in God," or "I can attract whatever I want." But it is a tremendously profitable chat that points a person in the direction of experiencing life as meaningful *on his own terms*. By speaking this way, a person can make smart predictions about what might feel meaningful to undertake, make sense of the tension between meaning and value, factor in idle pleasures and respites from meaning-making, calculate how much meaning he actually needs, and respond to the unremarkable truth that life has no single meaning with a robust "Yes, life is full of meanings!"

According to natural psychology, a person can act to change her circumstances if her circumstances provide her with too few opportunities for meaning and too few experiences of meaning. She can make sense of how her day feels and how her life feels and she can communicate with herself about meaning. She can reduce her reliance on big meanings by asserting that a mosaic of meaningful experiences that flow from her chosen idea of meaning and from her evaluation of life as worth something is meaning enough. She can reduce her defensiveness, increase her self-awareness, and change her habits of mind. Understanding that life is exactly and precisely this complicated, she can approach living intelligently rather than by dumbing it down.

By speaking honestly and clearly, an adherent of natural psychology can translate his value-driven impulses into concrete actions without second-guessing himself as to whether those actions have any ultimate value or whether they will make a real difference. Say, for example, that on a Tuesday it wells up in him to help feed certain hungry children. He does not have to make that the meaning of life because he understands that there is no such thing as the meaning of life. There are a multitude of life meanings—a multitude of psychological experiences of meaning—and he can invest a little of his human capital in his desire to help hungry children without having to invest everything.

In most traditional views, you need to know if what you are doing is considered higher than something else, in line with something else, or adherent to some sort of mandate, principle, or necessity. A follower of natural psychology understands that such worries are completely unnecessary. He knows that values compete, that values are contextual, that sometimes it is right to tell the truth and sometimes it is right to lie, that sometimes it is appropriate to sunbathe, and that sometimes it is appropriate to bear arms—that, in short, life is a puzzle made up of pieces that do not fit together perfectly and that can't fit together perfectly. He does not bother himself about some unreal ideal of perfection but rather asserts that he will put his personal puzzle together as sensibly, mindfully, and honorably as he can.

His self-chat about investing a little of personal capital in helping feed hungry children might sound like: "I understand that I can't be certain what effects my efforts will have. By the same token, I am convinced that if I feed those children over there, they will be less hungry. Now, I recognize that by feeding them and helping them survive, I may in fact be adding to the world's misery, because who knows if they will be good people, whether they will act in ways that increase or reduce goodness for others, and so on. That is, I understand that my feeding them is not a guarantee of anything with respect to increasing the amount of good in the world.

"I nevertheless feel like deciding that feeding hungry children, in the absence of powerful reasons not to do so, is a value I want to support. I do this with my eyes wide open with respect to life's absurdities and ambiguities. Because the argument I just presented to myself makes good sense to me, I believe that helping feed those children will provide me with the psychological experience of meaning. Even if it doesn't, however, I know that feeding those children aligns with my idea of what makes for a meaningful life. I'm predicting that it's going

Why Smart People Hurt

to feel meaningful, but even if it doesn't feel meaningful, I believe it is the right thing to do."

Yes, this self-chat is full of ironies and doubts. But an adherent smiles at those doubts and ironies, knowing that they come with the territory. He is well aware that the psychological experience of meaning is never guaranteed. In the end, he may find himself mildly or even gravely disappointed that his efforts to feed those hungry children did not provide the experience he had hoped they would provide. But he isn't surprised at such an outcome, and that result doesn't make him second-guess his approach to life. He knows that he only made a guess; he opted for a value he wanted to support and played a hunch about how it would feel to support that value. If it turns out that he guessed wrong, so be it.

He also recognizes that the meaningfulness of feeding starving children can change in the blink of an eye, meaning it is primarily a psychological experience. He might learn that he has an incurable cancer and not have the psychological space to think about anything but his own demise. He might learn that those children are the offspring of people he despises and discover that the thought of feeding them no longer interests him. He may learn that the food he is trying to provide them with is being diverted and now find the very idea of being of help losing a lot of its luster. That isn't to say that he might not still want to help, but it is also the case that he might indeed stop wanting to help.

He also recognizes that he is a tricky creature who must double-check his motives to make sure that he is telling himself the truth. Is he operating according to a value in wanting to feed those hungry children, or is he attracted to their mother? We are such wily, defensive creatures that we rarely put our cards face up on the table or make ourselves vulnerable by exposing our actual thoughts and desires, even to ourselves. By embracing natural psychology, he becomes aware of this human penchant for rationalization and self-delusion, and he includes among his menu of values the value of self-honesty.

Might he sometimes fool himself into believing that something he merely desires secretly has value? Of course he might. Say he really wants a lot of sparkly lights all over the outside of his house for exactly the sorts of reasons that a child might, because they would be pretty. Might he concoct a value to justify his desire and assert that the neighborhood would be safer with more illumination or that the beauty of light is its own justification? Of course he might. But, as an adherent of natural psychology, he knows to wonder about his motives even as he strings up those thousand lights. In the end, we might see him do the sort of thing that a self-aware person regularly does: he might string up those lights, stand back, smile a wry grin of comprehension, and take many of those lights down.

Natural psychology adherents recognize that the psychological experience of meaning is provoked in all sorts of ways and by all sorts of small moments: by the look of a ruined wall they pass, by the interplay of light and shadow on the sidewalk, by passing sights as they drive, by snatches of music coming from an open window, by the taste of something, by the feel of something, by the look of something. They are moved to the experience of meaning by winning, by flirting, by fantasizing, by feeling that they are liked and appreciated. They are moved to the experience of meaning when a meaning drain ends: when they find employment after a long lay-off, when they opt for recovery rather than addiction, when they stand up to a bully and watch him back down. Many experiences provoke the psychological experience of meaning.

An adherent of natural psychology recognizes that there are large meaning opportunities, meaning adventures, and meaning events like choosing a career, falling in love, manifesting potential, being of lifelong service, and so on. But she also understands that there are an infinite number of small meaning opportunities, meaning adventures, and meaning events as well, from making a personalized birthday card to seeing the sun reappear after a cloud passes by. Both small stimuli and big stimuli affect her experience of meaning. She fashions her idea of meaning from her experiences of meaning, she remembers to include the reality of this infinity of small events in her calculations, knowing that a given lost day may still be saved by virtue of nothing more dramatic than her catching sight of the last rays of sunlight.

An adherent of natural psychology knows that many challenges in the realm of meaning are coming. He understands that even though the sky is clear, a storm may be brewing. Therefore, he monitors his relationship to meaning in a daily way, not to find problems where none exist or to make trouble for himself but because he doesn't want to be blindsided by a meaning crisis. He learns how to be proactive in the realm of meaning. He learns how to think about, identify, and seize meaning opportunities and plug up meaning leaks. He monitors the idea of meaning that he has created and checks to make sure that he is not evaluating the meaningfulness of his life too harshly or too negatively. He does all of this in part to avoid the quiet growth of incipient meaning crises.

As he makes these calculations, evaluations, and decisions, he realizes that how he talks to himself makes a tremendous, even crucial, difference as to whether his efforts will bear fruit. Say he decides he might enjoy writing a novel that he's been contemplating writing. He guesses that writing it would feel meaningful, reasonable shorthand for "would evoke the psychological experience of meaning." But what if as he writes his novel, he badgers himself every day with self-talk that undermines his efforts? What will that badgering do to his experience of meaning and his ability to continue making meaning?

Say that at the end of every writing stint, he reads what he's written and observes, as is likely there on the page in front of him, a very mixed bag of goodness and badness. He could choose to say, "Some excellent bits there!" or he could choose to say, "Wow, what a load of crap!" By saying the latter, he is draining meaning from the enterprise of writing and aiming himself in the direction of quitting. Quite likely, his novel will no longer feel meaningful to him after some weeks of such self-bashing. In natural psychology, we consider choosing self-talk that serves our meaning needs to be a pivotal choice that we are obliged to make.

Just as he chooses to employ language that supports his meaning efforts, he chooses to employ language that aligns with his life evaluations. Say he evaluates life as worth living and feels reasonably sanguine that his current path is value driven and replete with excellent meaning opportunities. He should then likewise know that on a dull, dreary day, one of those days that everyone must endure, it will not pay him to say to himself, "Wow, I must be entirely mistaken about meaning—life looks to be pretty darn empty and meaningless!" When meaning is absent for a bit, it makes no sense to overthrow your positive evaluations about life. That is too dramatic a reaction to an ordinary, completely predictable meaning occurrence.

What if you can't help but judge life negatively? What if yesterday felt awful, today feels awful, and tomorrow is likely to feel awful too? What if you are poverty stricken, coughing up blood, incarcerated, alone, under siege, helpless, and hopeless? How absurd is it to ask you to make meaning and choose the meanings of your life? Don't you need medicine, money, and a friend more than some hard-nosed philosophy? Aren't you better off with a romantic movie, a pitcher of beer, and a dream of heaven rather than a demanding, soul-searching regimen? Doesn't natural psychology make little or no sense in your circumstances?

Actually, it may still make perfect sense. Natural psychology may in fact serve a person in these dire circumstances as well as or better than any other philosophy or religion does, given that it provides concrete strategies for increasing the experience of meaning and advocates actions of the sort that might make life more pleasant and more meaningful. It may be the case that someone who has a hard life is *exactly* the sort of person who would benefit from a philosophy that respects the hardness of reality and that proposes solutions, especially if that person is smart enough to understand the alternatives.

That isn't to say that there won't be days when all of us need meaning to amount to more than this, to something more profound and important, to something that better soothes us and helps us forget that we are bound to suffer and that we will cease to be. The natural psychological view does not controvert the facts of existence, and there will be days—many days—when even the staunchest heart wishes that it could. We boldly stare at the facts of existence—and on some days, each of us will blink. Adherents of natural psychology know that days like that are coming.

Rather than conceptualizing meaning as a lost object or as a reward for aligning with the universe, we see that it is something evoked in us by all manner of stimuli and that providing ourselves with those stimuli is a way—not a sure way but a good way—to experience life as meaningful. We choose those stimuli: dating, if intimacy provokes meaning; a slow walk across town, if the look of our town provokes meaning; a day of effort, if effort provokes meaning; watching a documentary film, if its subject provokes meaning; embarking on a bold adventure, if bold adventures provoke meaning; engaging in a value-based action, if value-based action provokes meaning. We do this even as the actual meaningfulness of a given belief, action, or activity shifts: we dance on, dealing with those inevitable shifts in meaning.

An adherent of natural psychology arrives at her ideas about meaning: she articulates what sort of thing she thinks meaning is, how it's influenced, how it's acquired, and what it isn't. She knows that she might experience meaning by spending the day in nature, but she also knows that she might not, since neither the idea of nature nor a given glen are meaningful in and of themselves. She knows this about meaning, and she isn't floored when a day in nature that she hoped would prove meaningful leaves her cold. He accepts that there are no unfiltered human experiences, no absolute meanings, and no guarantees.

First and foremost, she recognizes that life has no single or ultimate meaning. Life only has human meanings of the following sort: psychological experiences of meaning, fleeting moments of meaning, best guesses about meaning, constructed ideas about meaning, personal evaluations about the meaningfulness of life, and so on. This may strike her as terrible news or as wonderful news, but in either case, she is smart enough to know that it is the truth. She accepts this truth, embraces it, and makes considered choices in the realm of meaning—so as to give herself the best possible chance of crafting a life that feels authentic.

CHAPTER QUESTIONS

1. Describe in your own words why it is inevitable that meaning will shift.

2. How would you like to prepare yourself for these inevitable shifts?

3. What will be your first course of action when one of these shifts occurs?

4. If *authentic* is a word that appeals to you, how would you define it?

5. How might the practice of value-based meaning-making serve you in your efforts to meet the challenges we've been discussing?

18

EXERCISING YOUR BRAIN

In this chapter, I'd like you to do some thinking and some writing. You can do the following exercises in your mind's eye, if you like, and making just that effort will prove beneficial. It would be even better, however, if you engaged with these exercises and wrote out your answers. My goal is to have you experience how the principles and practices of natural psychology can help you deal with the smart challenges we've been discussing. I hope you find your own answers enlightening!

Paradigm Shift

To begin with, please describe what you see as the differences among the following three ideas:

- Seeking meaning

- Waiting for meaning to arrive

- Making meaning

Value-Based Meaning-Making

Your goal, if you would like to live authentically, is to make sufficient meaning and also to have that meaning align with your values. A sunny day, a bit of tomfoolery—anything might provoke the experience of meaning. That unbidden meaning is of secondary importance to the meaning that you make your way, in alignment with your values and your life purposes. The phrase value-based meaning-making stands for your thoughtful judgments about how you want to provoke the psychological experience of meaning, not as an imperative to provoke those experiences at any cost.

Ah, but the effort to make value-based meaning is such a serious and challenging one! It is not at all simple or straightforward to choose to do the right thing when you want to do the impulsive thing. It is ever so hard to honor your values when your liberty or your ease is at stake. It is seriously challenging to escape from or transcend your formed personality, with its habitual demands and its repetitive thoughts. It's quite a project even to know what values to support in the real-life situations that tumble before us one after another without pause.

Explain in your own words what the concept of making value-based meaning represents and what it would take to implement this concept in your life.

What Are Your Life Purposes, Values, and Principles?

What are you valuing? An ongoing practice of natural psychology is articulating your life purposes, your values, and your principles so you know what you intend to stand for and how you intend to live. By adopting the practice of regularly checking in on these three, you help point yourself in the direction of activities that you think will provoke value-based meaning.

Because of our ability to think, to form ideas, to evaluate, and so on, we find ourselves in the position of being able to come to conclusions about how we want to live our life and what actions we want to take in the service of those conclusions. We can decide that we want to uphold certain values, that we will endeavor to provoke meaning by upholding those values and not in other ways, that we can articulate and also alter and update our life purposes, and so on.

Take a little time to articulate your life purposes, your values, and your principles. Then consider (and write a bit) about the following: what actions have you taken in the service of your purposes, values, and principles?

Maintaining Your Life Purpose Vision

Let's say you have a picture in mind of exactly how you want to live your life. Where could you keep that picture so you could refer to it and have it remind you of your intentions? You might begin by creating a small life purpose statement that you use to help remind you of your life purpose vision. But let's say that you lose touch with, or lose track of, your life purpose vision. What might you do to regain touch and get back on track?

Psychological Subjectivity

Natural psychology takes as its starting point the reality of the human experience, the reality that we are not just acted upon, that we are not mechanical creatures who are programmed in a certain way and then play out our instructions. Rather, we are complicated creatures who experience life in a dynamic, interactive way. The best way to name this dynamism and this interactivity is psychological subjectivity.

Human life is a series of psychological experiences; a human being is a creature completely caught up in her own idiosyncratic, subjective, ever-changing personal reality. Given that this is our reality, how do you want to hold the fact that everything that *is* must be filtered through your psychological experience of life?

Defensiveness

Limiting our self-awareness is our defensiveness. Self-awareness gives us a chance at apprehending what we are up to, but our defensiveness limits that self-awareness. Our self-awareness is limited, sometimes severely, by our need to protect ourselves from confusing, unpleasant, or painful realities. That defensiveness is a human need for self-protection.

That term doesn't mean something completely negative. You might have a defensive need to discount the risks involved in doing something that you believe is valuable to do—you defensively discount those risks so as to allow yourself to *take* those risks. Like self-awareness and psychological subjectivity, defensiveness is a rich, rounded concept full of the same complexity that we see everywhere in the human condition.

Take a few minutes to describe the nature of your defensiveness—how does defensiveness manifest itself in you?

Habits of Mind

A concept to add to the ideas of psychological subjectivity, self-awareness, and defensiveness is the concept of habits of mind. Since it is just too difficult to reinvent ourselves every split second, we human beings are built to repeat ourselves without giving our current situation a lot of thought.

Through some combination of inheritance and living that, in natural psychology, we call our formed personality, we arrive pretty early on at our particular ways of saying things and doing things, our reflexive reactions to situations, our sets of beliefs and opinions, our prejudices and biases, our anxiety levels and thresholds, and our ways of looking at the world.

Once we are formed, we are hard-pressed to make changes to those habits of mind. In the context of natural psychology, part of an individual's work is to begin to update his habits of mind so that they serve the person he currently intends to be. Because we settle early on in life into hardened habits of mind that, along with our defensiveness, limit our self-awareness, our experience of life is more mechanical than it might be if we were less defensive and more open in our thinking.

Please describe as best you can how you would like to update your habits of mind.

Your Idea of Meaning

Natural psychology helps us understand that we can let go of our debilitating talk about the meaning of life and the purpose of life and can concentrate instead on creating a life that matches our vision of principled living.

We craft a smart, functional *idea* of meaning to deal with the fact that meaning is primarily a mere psychological experience, and we rally around our idea of meaning rather than pining for the experience of meaning. This is an amazing step forward for each individual and also a tremendous step forward for our civilization, since it is the value-based meaning-makers who do civilization's good work.

See if you can put into words your idea of meaning based on the concepts we've been chatting about. How do you want to hold the idea of meaning?

The Primacy of Available Personality

You have an original personality about which you will never really know enough, a formed personality that limits your freedom and increases your defensiveness, and an amount of available personality that is your current measure of freedom and self-awareness.

Discuss the idea of using your available personality in the service of value-based meaning-making in the context of this three-part personality model: unknowable original personality, limiting formed personality, and current available personality.

Investing Meaning

Feel in your body the difference between doing something versus investing meaning in something—that is, versus making a commitment because you believe that your choice is a value-based choice with the potential to make you feel proud of your efforts, that matches your idea of how life should be lived, and that may even provoke the psychological experience of meaning.

Describe in your own words what making a meaning investment signifies.

Meaning Opportunities

There is a difference between needing something to feel meaningful (or needing something to provoke the psychological experience of meaning) versus viewing something as a meaning opportunity because you have the hunch that it matches your vision of life and your idea of meaning.

Please describe what you see as the difference between *needing* something to feel meaningful versus looking at something as a meaning opportunity.

Boring or Difficult Work

Let's say that something you are doing is in the service of meaning but doesn't feel all that meaningful (that is, doesn't manage to provoke the psychological experience of meaning). Describe how you want to be with this situation so you are able to do this necessary work even though you aren't getting the payoff of the psychological experience of meaning.

Meaning Neutral

We use the phrase meaning neutral to stand for the idea that we do not need the psychological experience of meaning at all times, that some portion of the time we can operate in meaning neutral, and that the amount of meaning time and meaning neutral time each of us requires is for each of us to determine.

For one person, two hours of creating followed by eight hours of meaning neutral time followed by two hours of relating and intimacy may amount to a day that feels completely meaningful. Another person may have very different needs and very different requirements. Consider, and write about, the following questions:

1. How would you describe the idea of meaning neutral in your own words?

2. How many minutes or hours of active meaning-making do you think you need in a day for that day to feel satisfactory? Does that depend on how successful your meaning-making efforts were? What else might it depend on?

3. How would you describe the difference between spending some of your day in meaning neutral versus taking a vacation from meaning?

Choosing Meaning over Mood

An awful lot of people check in with themselves about what mood they're in but spend much less time checking in with themselves about doing something that matters to them. Can you see some advantages to focusing more on doing the things that matter to you rather than on keeping track of what mood you're in? We've chatted about the idea of allowing yourself to remain in meaning neutral for portions of the day. What do you think of the idea of remaining in mood neutral? Can you see mood neutrality as something you might want to cultivate?

Repairing Meaning

Meaning is infinite, and meaning is also fragile. This is no paradox, since we are talking about a phenomenon that only exists because of the peculiarities of human consciousness. A chair is a chair even if the human race disappears. But meaning, since it is an artifact of consciousness and only exists as a subjective experience and a human idea, vanishes with the species. Because of this truth, meaning repair is a pivotal natural psychology practice. Not only would meaning vanish with the extinction of the species—it can also vanish for an individual. This happens all the time. You do not want to let this happen!

Naturally it would be nice to be able to meet a meaning crisis in a split second rather than having to do the heavy lifting of actual repair. And sometimes you can. Sometimes you can bring yourself back just with a sigh, a laugh, or a tiny reminder. But there will be other times when the crisis is powerful and profound, when it feels less like a button popping off your shirt and more like the whole fabric ripping. Then you will need to pull out your meaning repair kit and carefully chat with yourself about what just transpired and how you intend to realign with your life purpose vision. To think about: what might you include in your personal metaphorical meaning repair kit?

Appropriate Distress

Someone with meaning needs will feel emotionally healthiest if she focuses on two areas, namely on making value-based meaning and on reducing her distress, insofar as that is possible. To use a simple analogy, she climbs the mountain but also tends to her blisters. As she climbs that mountain and as she tends to those blisters, she smiles a small knowing smile because she understands that she is living her life exactly as it ought to be lived.

However, she also understands perfectly well that she will sometimes *create* distress for herself because of the meaning investments she makes and the meaning opportunities she seizes. While she tries to minimize that distress, she nevertheless reminds herself that she has done this to herself and that she must live with some distress if she is to make herself proud. At the same time, she strives to *reduce* that distress as much as possible. This naturally leads to the idea of appropriate distress relief.

Think through this idea: that you want to *reduce* your distress but that you are also *creating* distress by virtue of the fact that you are actively making meaning.

Dealing with the Facts of Existence

It matters to a given human being whether he is born into this socioeconomic class or that one, whether his parents treated him well or poorly, whether his community lives peacefully or is continually at war, whether he is regularly healthy or regularly ill, whether the profession he would love to pursue is open to him or closed to him, and so on. Human life is nothing but psychological experiencing, and anything that affects our psychology—from growing up in a cult to growing up with a gold spoon in our mouth—matters.

All of that must be taken into account as we thoughtfully consider the sort of person we are, how we want to live, what we would like to change, and what about life we must accept. For example, which do you think would have the greatest impact on forming your personality: growing up poor, having mean parents, or being a minority member of your society? To consider: what are the current facts of your existence as they relate to the smart challenges we've been discussing?

Applying Natural Psychology Principles and Practices to Smart Challenges

If you think it would prove valuable and if you have the time and the energy, you might want to reread the first fifteen issue chapters with an eye to seeing how you might personally apply the principles and practices of natural psychology to each challenge. How, for example, might the idea of meaning neutral help you better deal with a boring job? How might the idea of making a new meaning investment prove a valuable technique for handling a smart gap? How might a morning meaning check-in serve to deal with incipient mania or other racing brain issues? And so on. If you feel up to it, this might prove to be the most valuable exercise of all.

CHAPTER QUESTIONS

1. Which of these exercises intrigued you the most and provided you with the most learning?

2. What exactly did you learn?

3. How will you implement what you learned?

4. To what extent do you need to update your personality in order to make those changes?

5. To what extent do you need to change the facts of your existence in order to make those changes?

19

A BLUEPRINT FOR SMART

Say you are born into the smartest 15 percent of the population and face many of the challenges that I've described—along with all of the other challenges of living. How might you proceed? That will depend in part on whether or not you agree with the vision of life described by natural psychology. If you agree with that vision, there's a reasonable (though, of course, imperfect) path to follow. Here is that vision reduced to its essentials. See if it makes sense to you.

You are born because nature makes creatures. You are one of nature's experimental models, like all creatures, and must deal with the peculiarities that come with being evolved rather than designed. This means that:

- You do not come with an on/off switch that allows you to quiet your mind at will. (You will have to deal with that.)

- You do not come with an immunity to mania, insomnia, or other racing brain ailments. (You will have to deal with that.)

- You do not come with a foolproof way of dealing with both the unreasonable and the reasonable thoughts that pester you. (You will have to deal with that.)

- You are not impervious to harsh treatment, cruel messages, ego bruises, false steps, disappointments, and the other blows that incline your formed personality in the direction of sadness and existential emptiness. (You will have to deal with that.)

- You come with a poorly calibrated danger warning system that produces too much anxiety far too often. (You will have to deal with that.)

In short, you are not immune to being human. You will have to deal with the idiosyncrasies of our species, idiosyncrasies that are often experienced as pain and distress. That pain and distress are regularly so severe that chemicals with powerful effects are used to mask and ameliorate them, as is the specialized talk known as psychotherapy. At the same time, reasonable ways of dealing with that pain and distress, ways rooted in the idea of making personal meaning, are too often ignored.

To begin with, you are born with an original personality made up of genetic messages, capacities, instincts, drives, awareness, and everything that you, a new human being, brings squirming into the rough and tumble of existence. This endowment may include a good mind, a touch of melancholia, a huge appetite, a clear sense of self, an innate stubbornness, a weakness for sweets, an easy smile, an ego that can be bruised, and so on. Your

Why Smart People Hurt

original personality includes aspects of your self that are hardwired and aspects of your self that are open—often too open by half—to the facts of existence. All of this, you come with into the world.

It would perhaps be nice to know the person you were meant to be—that is, the exact dimensions and qualities of your original personality—but that information is not available to you, which produces an odd life-long sore spot. You come into this world not as a blank slate but as a living, breathing human being who perhaps already has doubts and who perhaps already suspects the worse. The contours of that unknowable original personality matter; however, it is far more important that at some point you decide how you intend to live rather than remain pining for the person you might have been or ought to have been.

You are born, and then the world grabs you. You learn about doors slamming and neatly folding your hands and eating your peas and hiding out behind the hedge. You become the formed you, the child who daydreams or runs wild, the scared child, the helpful child, the beaten child looking for revenge, the child who associates with saints because her family is Catholic, the child whose natural intelligence makes her curious but whose schools dull her down. You become the child who, without giving it any thought, starts to dream of weddings or fast cars, great adventures or great sacrifices, novels to write or money to make. You start growing up.

You remain you and you become you—someone reminiscent of the original you but now a formed you. You become sexually active or sexually stifled, inclined to conform or inclined to rebel, with a focused love of physics or poetry or a diffuse interest in many things or no real passion for anything. You are driven in simple ways—aching for your friends' approval, hungry for a hamburger, craving victory on the basketball court—and driven in complex ways that are fueled by simmering doubts, failed undertakings, and the huge tension between what is and what you wish there was. You make it through your perhaps very dark teenage years and start to make predictions about your future, predictions called career choices and relationship choices.

It turns out that everything you do produces consequences. You ditch a test and end up changing majors. You meet a boy or a girl and end up in Bolivia. You have children early. You are completely embedded in reality, harboring dreams and feeling surprising distress, and no unseen friendly sprite exempts you from life. You have bills to pay. You need glasses. And throughout these years, a certain powerful self-interrogation commences: *Have I done the right thing? Why doesn't this feel more meaningful? What do I really believe? Is this all there is? How could I have been so stupid? What am I missing?* And so on.

Some of these pestering self-interrogations sound to your ear like therapy questions and some sound like spiritual questions. They are certainly not weird questions or neurotic questions, but it is hard for a person not schooled in natural psychology to accurately identify what sort of questions they are. They are the existential questions that arise before we understand our natural predicament and how to respond to life by making value-based meaning. Once we come to understand the nature of that response, we know how to matter, how to negotiate our days, how to meet meaning crises, how to reduce our distress, and how to make ourselves proud. Those questions quiet themselves or vanish entirely. Until then, however, we look very much like the next person, doing work that doesn't quite satisfy, dashing off for a spiritual quest or an affair, and convinced that meaning is hiding somewhere, maybe in the Himalayas, maybe just behind that door over there that we can't get open.

When we learn that meaning is not lost and that meaning can't be found and that meaning is exactly and precisely a subjective psychological experience that we can influence and even create, we suddenly stand in a new relationship to life. We stand up. And an odd thing happens. We become the beauty in life. We become beautiful to ourselves. To a smart person, this can sound like a soft, strange, flowery answer to the problem of existence, but it is our actual experience. Your loving heart was a beautiful thing while you loved. Your fierceness in defense of the defenseless was gorgeous. Your willingness to smile amounted to a small miracle. Reality has no mercy, but while you were the beauty in life, you were the beauty in life—all that merciless reality notwithstanding.

You may have come into this world already sad, already too knowing, already upset with reality. You may have arrived into a cold or careless home. You may find yourself indoctrinated in those first few seconds, belittled thereafter, and attacked by life. How can anyone be beautiful who begins by being attacked? Only a human being who, after a long journey down the usual broken and misleading paths, says, "Oh, I see how to be that beauty!"

You stand up, you update your personality, you mindfully decide on your next meaning investment, you stand open to meaning opportunities, and you feel a glow that I dare not write too much about without sounding ridiculous. But that glow is true; you are being true to yourself and, as a result, you feel beautiful.

You don't *have* to be beautiful. There is no one to tell you that you can't bellyache, whine, collapse, hate, hoard, criticize, or sneer instead—there are no arbiters of such matters. You can be as cruel and as miserable a person as you want to be. No fires of hell await you. There will be no retribution. You may even become president or chairman of the board by virtue of your cruelties. So be it. The universe allows you to be your worst self. Is that what you want? You can be meek and not like that; you can be rude and not like that; you can squander your intelligence on trifles and not like that; you can proceed through life by not doing what you should and not being who you should and not liking that. Or you can stand up and be the beauty in life, using your available personality and the freedom you possess in the service of your efforts to live life intentionally.

Over the past 150 years, we have taken the 19th-century ideal of truth, beauty, and goodness to the wood-shed and given it a necessary postmodern thumping. Truth got deconstructed. Beauty got ripped and shredded. Even second-rate relativistic arguments pounded goodness into submission. All this battering was completely necessary and absolutely right in its own way because we needed to look language in the eye and refuse to be seduced by its lure. But now, having done that appropriate analysis,

Why Smart People Hurt

we can refresh the ideal of truth, beauty, and goodness in a lovely reconstructive postmodern way that puts you and your meaning-making efforts front and center. You struggle to assert your truth based on your principles and your values—based, that is, on your goodness—and you become the beauty in life. Truth, beauty, and goodness return in the shape of a single human being.

What about tremendously taxing problems like a meaningless career, chronic sadness, a dissonant formed personality, daily money problems, cruel self-talk, and all the rest? What sort of answer is value-based meaning-making? What sort of answer is the exhortation to be the beauty in life? Isn't a better answer a comforting mysticism that predicts an idyllic future? Isn't a better answer chemicals that soothe you and alter your experience? Isn't a better answer fantasizing revenge, sleeping the pain away, or keeping frantic? What do you think? You get to decide.

You are not beautiful because there is some unseen force that made you in its image and holds you as an object of beauty. You are not an object of beauty. You are a *subject* of beauty. You know the difference between trying and not trying, and you know that it is beautiful to try. You *feel* that: you feel beautiful as you try, even if you are sweating buckets. This is a fierce beauty. This isn't the beauty of flower arrangements and classical columns. This is the beauty of pride and responsibility. This is the beauty of starting each day oriented in the direction of your life purposes. This is you mattering.

You've written five novels and none have been published. You've failed the bar exam six times. You teach in a school where no one listens or learns. Your mate belittles you. You have no one to love, and you doubt that love is in your future. Your father beat you. You have a chronic illness. You can't make ends meet. How can you possibly be the beauty in life in these circumstances? Why would you even want to be? Why bother? Shouldn't you hate life? Shouldn't you get what pleasure you can from cookies, from movies, from sleep? Isn't it asking too much of you to endure all this *and* make value-based meaning? Isn't that preposterous, ridiculous? You will have to decide.

If you agree with this vision of life, then you would proceed in the following pretty obvious way. You would engage in value-based meaning-making because you understand that such a way of life will do the very best job possible of upholding your values and principles, identifying your particular smart problems, making you proud, and reducing your distress. You accept that you can't do things that aren't available to you—you can't literally design and execute D-Day, reduce our species' way of expressing its self-interest as cruelty, repaint the ceiling of the Sistine Chapel, or have a good meal with your deceased loved ones—but that you can create a menu of meaning opportunities that actually matter to you and as a result stand in a different, better relationship to life, as one of the few people who wake up each day and can honestly say, "I have a decent sense of what matters to me, and today I get to live intentionally."

Likewise, by recognizing that we are an experimental model with many built-in challenges—from the way our anxiety early warning system overdoes it and gives

Why Smart People Hurt

us outlandish symptoms in the face of minimal danger to the way our racing brain feels so dangerous to us that we hold ourselves hostage to a forced calmness that feels like going through the motions—we can better surrender to and accept the fact that we are human, that we are not super-creatures, that we are bound to the facts of existence in simple ways that, however, do not need to cause us to badmouth ourselves and self-identify as bugs. We are neither gods nor bugs but members of a species that has evolved exactly as it has evolved and that is built to allow each member who cares to stand up to matter exactly as much as a human being can matter.

If your particular smart problem is that you were told you were brilliant too often and you got it into your head that you could do brilliant work without actually having to work, then now you make a meaning investment in actually working. If your particular smart problem is that your smartness (and all smartness) was disparaged by your society, your group, your parents, or your teachers, then you make a meaning investment in releasing old messages, healing old wounds, and standing up as a smart person. If your particular smart problem is that, being smart, you see reality a little too clearly and get chronically sad, you make a meaning investment in not adopting the customary label of *depression* but rather investigating your own case of sadness and what you intend to do to relieve that distress—say, by deciding that you will have meaning trump mood in your life and that you will pester yourself less about your mood and spend your days mattering.

If your day exhausts you without, however, providing you with much satisfaction, you use your smarts and make a meaning investment in discerning what must change. You discern what must change, and then you use your available personality to make those changes. If the challenge you identify is the super-large, super-powerful, super-painful one that nothing really can be made to matter—that you can't take your own menu of meaning investments and meaning opportunities seriously and you see through them instantly as merely created by you and not some universal imperative—then you stop everything and think through natural psychology's adamant request that you flip an inner switch and move from holding life as essentially meaningless to realizing that meaning is an infinite wellspring of a poignant humankind. You stop everything and reevaluate life as meaningful, in human terms and in human ways.

If people, including loved ones who have left you because of it, tell you that you are too arrogant, too inconsiderate, too full of yourself, and so on—and you can't help but agree, even if it irritates you to admit it—then you use your smarts and your available personality to make a meaning investment in updating your personality. If people, including you when you stare in the mirror, tell you that you have all this potential that you have never really manifested, then you use your smarts and your available personality to manifest that potential in ways that matter to you. You patiently face each challenge that I've identified and any other challenges that I haven't named but that you know exist.

It goes without saying that the challenges we've discussed do not vanish because you are able to keep your life purposes in mind, because you orient your life around

Why Smart People Hurt

making value-based meaning, or because you decide to make yourself proud by your efforts. Your mind will still race; incipient mania may still threaten you; the poignant distance between the smart work you would like to do and the work you are currently doing will still get you down. Life will still prove troubling. But side-by-side with these troubles is a picture of you as the beauty in life. I hope that you can see and feel this picture.

In the ways I've described, you become the beauty in life—the beauty in your own life. The 1.5 billion people in the smartest 15 percent of the world's population do not constitute an army for good, do not agree, and will never march together. In the aggregate, they do not amount to a beautiful thing. They are simply the smartest 15 percent of our species. But you can reduce your distress, meet your challenges as best as they can be met, and turn beautiful yourself by virtue of making the effort that you have always known to make—the effort to make yourself proud on a daily basis. Be smart, stand up, and live intentionally. We are members of a species who can do exactly that.

CHAPTER QUESTIONS

1. What special challenges do you experience by virtue of being smart?

2. How would you like to deal with them?

3. Which of those challenges appear to be in your power to handle, and which seem like they have to be lived with?

4. For those that must be lived with, what will you do to help yourself deal with their chronic and intractable nature?

5. What have I failed to cover that you know is an issue for you? How will you deal with it?

Why Smart People Hurt

ABOUT THE AUTHOR

Eric Maisel, PhD, is the author of more than 40 books in the areas of creativity, psychology, coaching, mental health, and cultural trends. He is a psychotherapist and creativity coach, and writes for *Psychology Today* and *Professional Artist Magazine* and presents workshops internationally. Visit him at *www.ericmaisel.com*.

TO OUR READERS

Conari Press, an imprint of Red Wheel/Weiser, publishes books on topics ranging from spirituality, personal growth, and relationships to women's issues, parenting, and social issues. Our mission is to publish quality books that will make a difference in people's lives—how we feel about ourselves and how we relate to one another. We value integrity, compassion, and receptivity, both in the books we publish and in the way we do business.

Our readers are our most important resource, and we appreciate your input, suggestions, and ideas about what you would like to see published.

Visit our website at *www.redwheelweiser.com* to learn about our upcoming books and free downloads, and be sure to go to *www.redwheelweiser.com/newsletter* to sign up for newsletters and exclusive offers.

You can also contact us at *info@rwwbooks.com*.

Conari Press
an imprint of Red Wheel/Weiser, LLC
665 Third Street, Suite 400
San Francisco, CA 94107